Nasr Abu Zaid

INDEX ON CENSORSHIP 4 1996

INDEX ON CENSORSHIP

Volume 25 No 4 July-August 1996   Issue 171

Editor & Chief Executive
Ursula Owen

Director of Administration
Philip Spender

Deputy Editor
Judith Vidal-Hall

Production Editor
Rose Bell

Fundraising Manager
Elizabeth Twining

News Editor
Adam Newey

Fundraising Assistant
Joe Hipgrave

Editorial Assistants
Anna Feldman
Philippa Nugent

Africa
Adewale Maja-Pearce

Eastern Europe
Irena Maryniak

Circulation & Marketing Director
Louise Tyson

Subscriptions Manager
Kelly Cornwall

Accountant
Suzanne Doyle

Volunteer Assistants
Michaela Becker
Laura Bruni
Kate Cooper
Ian Franklin
Madeleine Glover
Nevine Mabro
Nicholas McAulay
Mansoor Mirza
Albert Opoku
Grazia Pelosi
Dagmar Schlüter
Kate Smith
Sarah Smith
James Solomon
Katheryn Thal
Melissa Twyford
Saul Venit
Tara Warren
Predrag Zivkóvic

Directors Louis Blom-Cooper, Ajay Chowdhury, Caroline Moorehead, Ursula Owen, Peter Palumbo, Jim Rose, Anthony Smith, Philip Spender, Sue Woodford (Chair)

Council Ronald Dworkin, Amanda Foreman, Thomas Hammarberg, Clive Hollick, Geoffrey Hosking, Michael Ignatieff, Mark Littman, Pavel Litvinov, Robert McCrum, Uta Ruge, William Shawcross, Suriya Wickremasinghe

Patrons Chinua Achebe, David Astor, Robert L Bernstein, Harold Evans, Richard Hamilton, Stuart Hampshire, Yehudi Menuhin, Iris Murdoch, Philip Roth, Tom Stoppard, Michael Tippett, Morris West

Index on Censorship (ISSN 0306-4220) is published bi-monthly by a non-profit-making company: Writers & Scholars International Ltd, Lancaster House, 33 Islington High Street, London N1 9LH

Tel: 0171-278 2313
Fax: 0171-278 1878
E-mail:
indexoncensor@gn.apc.org
http://www.oneworld.org/index_oc/

Index *on Censorship* is associated with Writers & Scholars Educational Trust, registered charity number 325003

Periodicals postage (US subscribers only) paid at Newark, New Jersey. Postmaster: send US address changes to *Index on Censorship* c/o Mercury Airfreight Int/ Ltd Inc, 2323 Randolph Avenue, Avenel, NJ 07001, USA

Subscriptions 1996
(6 issues p.a.)
Individuals: UK £36, US $50, rest of world £42
Institutions: UK £40, US $70, rest of world £46
Students: UK £25, US $35, rest of world £31

© This selection Writers & Scholars International Ltd, London 1996
© Contributors to this issue, except where otherwise indicated

Printed by Martins, Berwick upon Tweed, UK

Cover design: Andrea Purdie

Photo credits: Front cover: Ian-Iraq war: An Iranian woman stands on top of a captured Iraqi tank/Kaveh Golestan; Back cover: Nasr Abu Zaid/The Independent/ David Rose

Australian committee Philip Adams, Blanche d'Alpuget, Bruce Dawe, Adele Horin, Angelo Loukakis, Ken Methold, Laurie Muller, Robert Pullan and David Williamson c/o Ken Methold, PO Box 825, Glebe NSW 2037, Australia

Danish committee Paul Grosen, Niels Barfoed, Claus Sønderkøge, Herbert Pundik, Nils Thostrup, Toni Liversage and Björn Elmquist, c/o Claus Sønderkøge, Utkaervej 7, Ejerslev, DK-7900 Nykobing Mors, Denmark

Dutch committee Maarten Asscher, Gerlien van Dalen, Christel Jansen, Chris Keulemans, Wieke Rombach, Mineke Schipper and Steven de Winter, c/o Gerlien van Dalen and Chris Keulemans, De Balie, Kleine-Gartmanplantsoen 10, 1017 RR Amsterdam

Norwegian committee Trond Andreassen, Jahn Otto Johansen, Alf Skjeseth and Sigmund Strømme, c/o NFF, Bydøy allé 21, N-0262 Oslo, Norway

Swedish committee Gunilla Abrandt and Ana L Valdés, c/o Dagens Nyheter, Kulturredaktionen, S-105 15 Stockholm, Sweden

USA committee Rea Hederman, Peter Jennings, Harvey J Kaye, Susan Kenny, Jane Kramer, Radha Kumar, Jeri Laber, Gara LaMarche, Anne Nelson, Faith Sale, Michael Scammell, Wendy Wolf

Former Editors: Michael Scammell (1972-81); Hugh Lunghi (1981-83); George Theiner (1983-88); Sally Laird (1988-89); Andrew Graham-Yooll (1989-93)

EDITORIAL

Faith and the millennium

N̲O SOCIAL OBSERVER at the beginning of this century would have
predicted the strength of religion at the end of it. Why faith has
survived, and whether materialism, rationalism and science have lost their
appeal in a century in which some of the worst horrors against humanity
have been inflicted are two of the many questions *Index* asks in this issue.

In Islam, faith and revelation have more than survived. Virtually
unacknowledged by the outside world, Islamic scholarship, debate and
political activity have been experiencing a modernising renaissance on an
extraordinary scale, in which, amongst other things, revelation and reason
are seen to be not incompatible. Meanwhile, the West, preoccupied with
Islamic fundamentalism, has not always understood that the majority of
committed Muslims belong to the moderate mainstream.

This does not mean that fundamentalisms of all kinds are not a
continuing danger. In Iran, where the gulf between hardline clergy and
reformist thinkers is widening, Abdolkarim Sorush's lectures on separating
state and religion are repeatedly broken up by militants. By applying
contemporary textual criticism to the Quran, the Egyptian scholar Nasr
Abu Zaid has been seen to challenge religious orthodoxy and forced to
flee his country. Meanwhile, in a dangerously divided Israel, the murder
of Yitzak Rabin has highlighted the strength of the tribal/religious
constituency, with its deep commitment to religious law. In the USA,
where the Christian Right are, as Darryl Pinckney argues, 'extremists as
lovers of conformity', extremism of a kind underpins the most revered
foundations of the nation. And wherever the rhetoric of fundamentalism
merges with nationalist fervour, a dangerous cocktail results.

In a fragmented world of belief, no one 'ism', sacred or profane, is likely
to dominate successfully. But what this issue of *Index* and its in-depth file
on Saudi Arabia seem to show is that, whether we like it or not, the
immediate hope of countering religious extremism lies not with
secularism but with modernisers from within. ❑

• *We encourage our readers to write to us, and hope this issue in particular will
provoke letters (please keep them short)*

contents

in the news

• **In Ireland**, veteran crime reporter Veronica Guerin was gunned down in Dublin shortly after interviewing a local mafia boss (see p88), while in Russia, Chechnya and Ukraine, organised crime has taken its revenge on three more journalists by murdering them following reports on mafia activities.

• **Pope John Paul II** found himself censored by his own bishops on a visit to Germany in June. They excised from his homily — delivered at the stadium built by Hitler for the 1936 Olympics — a passage praising the Catholic hierarchy's 'glorious' record of resisting Nazism.

• **The world's last Yiddish daily**, Paris-based *Unzer Wort*, disappeared from the scene at the end of June. End of almost 50 years in publishing; death of the language of European Jewry.

• **Belarus marked the tenth anniversary** of Chernobyl on 26 April with an official 'mass' demonstration of 5,000 bused-in by their work places, and an unofficial one of 50,000 organised by the opposition which was broken up by baton-wielding police.

• **The 'electronic chador'**, the latest fashion in designer graphics, has come to the aid of the Islamic Republic of Sudan. This neat little electronic gismo can be conveniently slipped into place on screen by the godly censors when the *décolletage* or hemlines in the ever popular Egyptian films and soaps are just too much — or too little — for the muftis. Whatever would Coco have said?

• **Computer retouching** in imported magazines has caught on with a vengeance in Saudi Arabia. Modest hemlines are seamlessly — almost

— tacked on to Givenchy or St Laurent fashion items; under-dressed diplomatic wives at receptions are given the treatment. Strangely, offending necklines and sleeveless tops are still remedied by more traditional methods: an army of men with black marker pens.

• **Britain's ban** on TV and radio ads for organisations whose aims are, according to the Radio Authority, 'of a political nature' — such as *Index on Censorship* and Amnesty International — has been reaffirmed by the standing committee on the new Broadcasting Bill: it voted 12 to nine not to change the crucial wording to 'of a party-political nature'.

• **Sales of Coca-Cola** look set to plummet in Kuwait after the drinks giant produced an ad showing a Muslim prostrated in prayer before the company's logo. Local columnist Fouad Hashem demanded a boycott thundering: 'Let them go to hell with their drink.'

• **Québec's separatist government** has voted to bring back the so-called language police, whose task is to track down English-only signs in the province, and to make sure that on bilingual signs the French words are more prominent than the English translation.

• **The Communications Decency Act** failed to clean up the Internet, so here comes PICS (Platform for Internet Content Selection), a sort of DIY censorship kit which allows each user to decide what he or she shouldn't be allowed to see. Further proof, if any were needed, of the truly democratising nature of the medium (see p132).

Spot the join...(see Saudi Arabia)

• **The honorary consul** in Rangoon, James Leander Nichols (65), was found all but dead in his cell in Burma's Insein prison on 22 June to which he had been transferred the night before after having disappeared from sight since his arrest on 18 May. He died one hour later in hospital. His offence? To have possessed no less than 'two fax machines and several telephone lines' in his office. He was also a close friend of Aung San Suu Kyi and it was he who originally pressed her to return to Burma and take on the SLORC (see p179).

• **Pakistan's fundamentalist** Jamaat-e-Islami party has announced its intention of 'plunging into the battle' against Benazir Bhutto's government. A confrontation between Islamists protesting against corruption and the cost of living and security forces in Rawalpindi on 24 June left four of the former dead.

• **Not content** with continuing its military onslaught on the Kurds, Turkey is about to ban the pro-Kurdish Turkish Workers' Party, reports the Anatolian Press Agency. On 24 June, some 200 demonstrators protesting the proposal were wounded in clashes with security forces. Twenty-four members of the party were arrested on the same day for 'insulting the national flag'.

• **The European Union's united front** against the *fatwa* on Salman Rushdie was shattered at the end of June, when serious differences emerged between France, Italy and Spain who supported a compromise deal in which the EU would accept the 'validity and irrevocability' of the *fatwa* in exchange for written assurances from the authorities in Iran, and Britain, said to be reluctant to trust any such assurances. The International Rushdie Defence Committee has condemned outright any such compromise: to accept the *fatwa*, they say, 'would establish the dangerous precedent of cultural relativism; that the right to freedom of speech can be abnegated by religious dictate'.

Rushdie himself, meanwhile, met the Dutch foreign minister, Hans van Mierlo. The latter stated categorically that the EU 'should not agree to any phrasing that would seem to accept the death verdict over Rushdie'.

Corrigendum 'Israel must speak to Hamas' (*Index* 3/1996) The suicide bomb on 19 October 1994 was in Dizengoff Street, Tel Aviv, not Jerusalem. We apologise for this error in transmission

• **US President Clinton**, ever eager to harness the tide of electoral fortune, tried hard to bend the agenda for the Group of Seven (G7) meeting in Lyon to his advantage. With the summit coming so soon after the bomb in Dhahran, Saudi Arabia, that killed 19 American servicemen, the assembled governments were bounced into preparing a joint statement condemning terrorism — rather than getting to grips with the more contentious scheduled issue of unilateral US trade embargoes against Cuba, Libya and Iran.

Resentment against the Cuba Liberty and Democracy Solidarity Act (the so-called Helms-Burton law), which threatens reprisals against non-US companies doing business in Cuba, has been running high among Washington's major trading partners for some months. The most punitive provisions of that law are due to come into effect on 1 August, when US citizens who owned property in Cuba before 1959 will be able to sue foreign companies which 'traffick' in US property confiscated after the 1959 revolution in Havana. The law has been condemned as high-handed and counter-productive everywhere outside the US; the other six G7 members presumably felt that there were more pressing things to talk about than terrorism.

Clinton's reluctance to lock horns with his foreign allies is not surprising. The Cuban government's crackdown against opposition activists in Havana continues unabated and, with an election to be fought in November, Clinton is under intense pressure from the powerful anti-Castro lobby in Miami and New York to keep the sanctions regime in place, regardless of whether it is effective or not.

Now another sanctions bill, proposed by senator Alfonse D'Amato and designed to penalise foreign petroleum companies that do business with two of America's other foreign policy bogeymen, Iran and Libya, has substantially raised the stakes. The D'Amato bill was originally modelled on Helms-Burton, but a weakened version passed unanimously by the House in June is less draconian, allowing sanctions only against companies making new investments in those countries' oil or gas industries.

D'Amato, for one, was quick to point to the Dhahran bomb as conclusive evidence of the need to deal effectively with 'terrorist states' — code for Iran. Since D'Amato also heads the Dole election campaign team, it's unlikely that Clinton is going to allow himself to be outflanked by the enemy on this issue.

• **Iran's Ansarallah** — an armed offshoot of the Ansar-e Hezbollah and the Islamic Republic's answer to the storm troopers of Nazi Germany — are striking terror into the hearts of the country's academic establishment. Under the command of Ayatollah Ahmad Janatti, one of the most prominent hardline clerics close to Supreme Guide, Ayatollah Ali

Khamenei, the 5,000- to 7,000-strong force is drawn from young, illiterate peasants, trained to crush any views or behaviour considered 'un-Islamic' by the regime. Under the protection of the office of the Supreme Guide, equipped with powerful motorcycles and armed with knives, iron bars and other so-called 'non-lethal' weapons, they break up lectures, threaten teachers and intimidate students (see p165).

• **China's nationwide** anti-crime drive, nicknamed 'Strike Hard', has struck especially hard in Xinjiang Uighur Autonomous Region, in the northwest of the country. Since the campaign began in April, at least 4,700 Uighur Muslims — the largest of the region's 47 ethnic groups — are thought to have been detained.

China blames a series of 'violent and terrorist cases' by Uighur national separatists for the crackdown. Since the start of the year, the region has been rocked by 'splittist' activity, including bombing campaigns, the assassination of a pro-Communist mullah, Akensu Sidike, and clashes with police in Wensu and Kuga districts. Violence has continued in spite of the Chinese initiative. Muhidin Mukhlissi, spokesman for the Xinjiang separatist Revolutionary Front of East Turkestan, reports street fighting in late May that left 20 dead in Turfan and Karami.

China's crackdown has been ferocious. Troops have been sent in to suppress uprisings and tighter border controls have been implemented to curb weapon smuggling and the import of subversive propaganda from sympathetic Uighur groups in neighbouring Kazakhstan. China has also put pressure on other Central Asian states to act against Uighur separatists operating from exile.

Another focus of the Xinjiang campaign has been 'illegal religious activity'. In April, tighter rules governing Islamic publications were announced: the import of Islamic books, periodicals, audio- and videotapes from abroad are banned; locally published scriptures and interpretative works must be submitted for prior censorship.

In May, the target switched to the *talipu* (underground religious study groups), long seen as a potential breeding ground for splittist activity. A ban was placed on the construction of new mosques, mullahs were prohibited from preaching outside their mosques and 10 unauthorised places of worship were closed down. 'Freedom of religion is not freedom of religious belief,' the official *Xinjiang Daily* stated. 'It does not mean you can do whatever you want.'

The Chinese press has lauded the success of the campaign, citing the confiscation of books, the arrest of 'hooligans' and the prosecution of at least one man, Abuduwayiti Aihemaiti, for writing and distributing 'reactionary propaganda'. Unrest continues, however, and in the latest reports China speaks of the need to erect a 'wall of steel' around Xinjiang.

• **Dateline Bahrain** 18 June: 'Thirteen small bombs. Nobody hurt' read the agency despatch. No big deal, coming as it did hot on the excitement earlier in the month (3 June) when Bahrain's emir of 30 years' standing, Sheikh Issa Bin Salman al-Khalifa, announced the scotching of an Iranian-backed coup plot to a hastily summoned local press corps. But evidence enough that the emir is not rid of the unrest that has plagued him for almost two years (see *Index* 2/1995). And with local merchants wringing their hands, foreign investment 56 per cent down on last year and a bigger turnover in bombs, demonstrations and sabotage of key power installations since the beginning of this year, the ruler of the region's main offshore banking and service centre — home, too, to the US Fifth fleet — is not anxious to have it known that his egregious head of security, one Ian Henderson, an ex-colonial British copper, is still not in command of the situation.

Which is why, the opposition alleges, the emir and his press corps have taken control themselves: hatching the plots, writing the stories and carefully orchestrating the ensuing press and TV coverage.

Advised at the beginning of the year by his newly appointed PR firm that disclosure was the best policy, Sheikh Issa seems to have gone for overkill. Blanket coverage of the 'plot' in the wholly subservient local press almost before the microphones had been turned off in the press conference summoned to disclose the plot; live 'confessions' on television the following day; massive arrests among the Shia community; and a fury of anti-Shia propaganda in the days that followed.

Meanwhile, the government does nothing to address the modest demands of the opposition back in December 1994 — a return to the 1973 constitution and the elected assembly dissolved by Sheikh Issa in 1975 — and the toll has risen to at least 24 Shia 'martyrs' and up to 2,000 prisoners. Encouraged by its minister of information, the local press whips up communal tension, ensuring that violent protest continues. 'Nothing harms the Gulf states, or undermines their stability, more than their information ministers,' commented the London-based *al-Quds al-Arabi*'s columnist.

• **Germany's** Chancellor Kohl pulled out all the stops for Tibetan independence at the end of June by publicly defending a parliamentary resolution that accused China of committing cultural genocide in the Himalayan nation. 'The German parliament is not subject to censorship,' he proclaimed, after protests from Beijing. He rather spoiled things, however, by adding that he nevertheless supports the 'one China' policy. After all, he said, 'China always believed in the unity of the German nation and...supported German unification.' ❏

MICHAEL WILLIAMS

Polling for partition

Peace has confirmed the ethnic divisions forged by war; elections in September are likely to legitimise their leaders and warlords

SARAJEVO in June 1996 is a city transformed. The streets are crowded, pavement cafes have appeared on virtually every street, trams and buses are running, some of them new, and the utilities have been restored. Not quite 24 hours a day but enough to make the running of a water tap or the flick of an electricity switch seem a miracle to survivors of the longest siege since World War II. In the brilliant summer sunshine the war already seems distant to the outsider. Even to the citizens of a city whose name has twice in a century been indelibly written into the history books, looking up at the hills from which Bosnian Serbs mercilessly rained down artillery and sniper fire seems past history; and it probably is. The charred remains of the National Library remain a haunting reminder of the devastation wreaked upon the city in the ugliest challenge to European civilisation since 1945.

Now the city is reunited, but not reconciled. For the most part the Serbs have left the suburbs that had to be returned to the Bosnian government under the Dayton agreement, and, disturbingly, there are almost daily reports that those who remain are subject to harassment and intimidation from Muslims who increasingly appear to have adopted the selfishness of their erstwhile enemies. Much of this comes from refugees, victims of ethnic cleansing in eastern Bosnia. Their own home towns — Visegrad, Foca, Zvornik and more recently Srebrenica — are now ethnically pure and festooned with portraits not only of Radovan Karadzic, president of the Serb Republic, but also of Arkan, the militia leader who pioneered ethnic cleansing, first in Croatia and then in Bosnia. The famous bridge at Visegrad still bears its Turkish inscriptions, silent witness to the hundreds of Muslims who were murdered and thrown from it in the cruel summer of 1992.

IN JUST over two months from now, on or before 14 September, the people of Bosnia-Hercegovina will go to the polls, nine months to the day that the Dayton Agreements were formally signed in Paris last December. Those agreements scheduled to last 12 months were always dictated not by the measure of the tasks that confronted the international community in trying to rebuild Bosnia, but purely by US electoral considerations. President Clinton, having decided finally in the summer of 1995 to intervene diplomatically and militarily, was determined that results must be shown by the time he sought re-election in November 1996. Correspondingly, it was yet another demonstration of European political weakness that they accepted a timetable in Bosnia driven purely by US domestic political considerations. As a result, scant time has been given for more moderate political opinions to emerge in all three communities, or for the people of Bosnia to witness the results of economic reconstruction and harness a peace dividend.

By contrast, in Cambodia in 1992-3 the UN Transitional Authority (UNTAC) had 15 months to organise a similar exercise and did so only after the return of refugees and after minimal standards of freedom of movement and of the media had been obtained. Fortunately, that exercise did not involve US troops whose country's intervention in Bosnia has simultaneously delivered peace, but at the same time frozen the political status quo, itself a result of ethnic cleansing. Thus, the Dayton Accord recognised the Republika Srpska (the Bosnian Serb Republic), as a legitimate political entity, an ethnically pure statelet founded on the physical liquidation or expulsion of all minorities, a chilling precedent for Europe at the end of the century. Small wonder that in the endless speeches and events that commemorated the fiftieth anniversary of the defeat of fascism, no statesman dared refer to Bosnia.

The Dayton Agreements, in a mix of realpolitik and idealism, also provided for the rebuilding of a new Bosnia and the construction of new federal institutions. But it did so on the basis of recognising two entities, the aforementioned Serb Republic and the Muslim-Croat Federation. This latter political formation, the result of a previous US intervention — the Washington Agreement of March 1994 — groups another ethnically pure statelet, the Croat Republic of Herzeg-Bosna with the rump Bosnian Republic based in Sarajevo. The latter, while Muslim dominated, does to its credit still tolerate a degree of media pluralism and many thousands of Serbs and Croats who constitute about 30 per cent of its population. The

Serb and Croat statelets are more than 99 per cent ethnically pure.

In itself, the logic behind Dayton was not doomed to failure, and, even at this late hour, there may still be some hope that it is not. But it can only succeed if minimal standards of democratic behaviour are introduced and a greater degree of pluralism and tolerance encouraged and sustained in all communities. Recognising the Republika Srpska, which the much maligned United Nations refused to do, would not have been so bad had it been accompanied by a political strategy designed to prise the Serb population away from the clutches of Radovan Karadzic and General Mladic, whose crazed behaviour has earned for Serbs an almost universal opprobrium. Instead, not only are these two indicted war criminals still free men, but they retain the levers of political and military power in the Serb Republic: in mid May, when the hapless prime minister of the Serb Republic, Rajko Kasagic, was dismissed for exhibiting a degree of independence from his president, Karadzic promptly dismissed him. That step was described by he high representative charged with implementing the civil side of Dayton, Carl Bildt, as a 'coup d'état'. The problem for Dayton and the prospects of democracy in Bosnia is that it was a successful coup d'état.

If the absence of media freedom and freedom of movement was not crippling in itself, the mocking presence of Karadzic cruelly undermines the expectations for September's election. In the first place it makes the emergence of more tolerant politicians in the Serb Republic unlikely and almost confirms that the psychiatrist's party will sweep the board there. Secondly, it encourages the likelihood that other ethnic warlords will triumph electorally in the Croat and Muslim communities, hardly a basis upon which to construct a new federal Bosnia. The recent Dayton review conference in Florence on 13-14 June called once again for the mad doctor's removal from political life, but only his physical arrest and deportation to the war crimes tribunal in The Hague is likely to contain his poisonous influence. Daily the commanders of 60,000 of the world's best trained, equipped and armed troops pronounce themselves incapable, unwilling or fearful of the consequences of such an act; a view which, if it prevailed in a domestic jurisdiction, would excuse police from the dangers of arresting armed criminals.

NATO has met with considerable military success in implementing the Dayton accords, but that could not have been otherwise. Most Serb politicians were deliriously happy to learn that the US and European

ZORAN FILIPOVIC

National Library, Sarajevo: haunting monument to European barbarity

democracies were willing for NATO troops to separate them from Muslims and Croats. What they did not want to see, and here, alas, they have been largely successful, is the rigorous implementation of the civil side of the Dayton accords. While Carl Bildt has been much criticised in this regard, it has been the unwillingness of IFOR (the NATO implementation force) to move beyond the narrowest interpretation of its mandate that has frozen the status quo of ethnic partition. Thus, when the Sarajevo suburbs were torched by Serb looters in March, IFOR's presence was stunningly absent. Similarly, NATO patrols stand by as Karadzic's motorcade glides effortlessly back to Pale, his hilltop capital, from gambling forays at the Hotel Metropole in Belgrade. How is one to answer the criticism of one commentator in the *New York Times*, who described IFOR's policy as having moved 'from the inexplicable to the repellent'.

Clearly the international community, and above all the USA, is determined to hold elections in September come what may. If the earth needs to be declared flat in the process, so be it. That not a single refugee has been able to return home other than to areas where his or her ethnic community prevail, that the Croat Republic retains its neo-fascist leanings and the Serb Republic would not need to learn lessons from North Korea in terms of media control, that the distinguished former Bosnian prime minister, Haris Silajdzic, can be beaten around the head with an iron bar by Muslim zealots at a campaign rally, none of this daunts the architects of Dayton or leads them to a moment's hesitation about holding elections in September. For without elections there is no clear exit strategy and President Clinton remains determined not to go to his polls in November without having cleared a decisive hurdle in Bosnia.

Herein lies one of the most painful consequences of the Bosnian conflict from its outbreak in May 1992. If it were not tragedy enough that communities that had lived alongside each other for decades descended into a nightmare of fratricidal conflict, that conflict has in turn weakened and sapped the moral fibre of all the international actors who have sought to intercede. The EU, having demonstrated its ineptitude in the Croatian war of 1991, was happy to force the UN into Bosnia against the expressed recommendation of its secretary-general, Boutros-Ghali, who could see no place for a traditional peacekeeping force when there was no peace to keep. The UN, having been unceremoniously evicted in 1995, has been replaced by a military force three times its size deployed on both sides of the confrontation line which, in a six-month deployment, has so far suffered less casualties than the New York police department in a week. This unwillingness to undertake the slightest risk, the predominant concern among IFOR's US commanders, renders implementation of the civil side of Dayton a Sisyphean endeavour. But it can hardly be a triumph for NATO if its first military engagement ends up in a Cyprus-type solution for Bosnia. When has partition ever been a lasting solution to communal conflict? Cyprus aside, one would have thought that the lessons of Ireland, Palestine and India were eloquent enough.

It is above all the Organisation for Security and Cooperation in Europe (OSCE), still a child in institutional terms, that has to bear the heavy responsibility for supervising the September elections. Under the chairmanship of the Swiss foreign minister, Flavio Cotti, it has struggled to keep some institutional independence with regard to the elections under intense American pressure. Ironically, the OSCE only has the job because of Washington's visceral dislike of the UN. One of the things the UN has time and time again demonstrated is precisely its capability in organising elections, as Namibia in 1989 and Cambodia in 1993 strikingly demonstrated. What the UN achieved, above all, in Cambodia was the creation of a democratic space in which newspapers and NGOs flourished for the first time in Cambodia. In addition, by the very act of holding the elections and achieving an almost 90 per cent turnout, Pol Pot and the Khmer Rouge were marginalised politically.

Tragically, that has not happened in Bosnia. Indeed, as a recent meeting of journalists I chaired in Sarajevo highlighted, it is above all journalists who do not enjoy any freedom of movement. Even with NATO's substantial military presence, no Bosnian journalist could venture into the Croat or Serb statelets without fear. No local NGOs are able to operate across confrontation lines. What democratic space there is exists wholly in the territory of the Bosnian republic and even here it is under pressure from the SDA (Party of Democratic Action), the increasingly authoritarian ruling party of President Alija Izetbegovic. The UN High Commission for Refugees has laboured ceaselessly to breach the walls of partition, organising buses across confrontation lines and visits by refugees to their former homes, but with little real success and, so its officials claim, with minimal assistance from NATO.

There is always the distant hope that some 'good guys' will emerge in the polls. Some observers place hope in Haris Silajdzic's Party for Bosnia-Hercegovina, which may do reasonably well in Bosnian government territory. But it will be to the enduring cost of the international community that it has signally failed in changing the profoundly undemocratic structures of the Serb and Croat statelets. Critically, the implementation of the Dayton agreements has not done enough to create the space in which 'good guys' could emerge as meaningful political actors. How could this be otherwise, some would argue, when President Milosevic of Serbia and President Tudjman of Croatia were the West's main interlocutors in bringing about the Dayton agreement. As one Sarajevan friend commented: 'In 1995 we had the hope of peace. This year we have peace and no hope.' I can only hope he is not right. ❏

Michael Williams was director of information for the UN Protection Force in the former Yugoslavia (UNPROFOR) in 1994-5. He was previously deputy director of Human Rights for the UN Transitional Authority in Cambodia (UNTAC) in 1992-3. He is now a senior fellow at the International Institute for Strategic Studies, London, and has recently returned from a visit to Bosnia

ROMANA DOBNIKAR-SERUGA

OFiaRa SERWiSv pRaSoWeGo·

MONIKA JAWOROWSKA/RZECZPOSPOLITA

RIP: died in the service of the press

In peace as in war

The Council of Europe has deferred Croatia's application for membership citing its 'lack of respect for the freedom of the press'. But the peace-time media in other Balkan republics is faring no better

O N 15 FEBRUARY this year, the Belgrade commercial court annulled the privatisation of Studio B television, even though its 1991 privatisation had been carried out to the letter of the laws then in force. Belgrade's only independent channel had won the hearts of its public for its coverage of the war: Studio B was the only Belgrade channel to broadcast uncensored reports from the battlefields of Bosnia. But it had invited the anathema of the regime by supporting the demonstration against the dismissal of 1,000 journalists working in state television in January 1993.

The city council took control and promised to turn Studio B into a 'modern, sophisticated and decent' channel. What they meant by 'decent' was immediately apparent when the bulk of the following day's news was devoted to the ruling party to the exclusion of the opposition.

Studio B was the latest in the line of closures and government take-overs that have characterised Slobodan Milosevic's handling of the media. The daily, *Borba*, disappeared in December 1994, the Kragujevac daily *Svjetiost* in 1995. Only Radio B 92, the weeklies *Nin* and *Vreme* and the Beta press agency survive to tell the tale.

To say that Milosevic 'censors' his journalists gives a false impression: there are other ways of silencing them. Insubordinate journalists are dubbed 'betrayers of the Serb nation', 'hirelings of the opposition' or even 'agents of foreign powers'. The regime also uses more sophisticated, but just as effective, methods to get rid of them: journalists' access to frequencies is limited, their supply of newsprint is cut, prices are fixed, advertisers are pressured into withdrawing their business, independent journalists are attacked in the official media and prosecuted for 'word-crime'.

Milosevic's latest campaign against the independent media was carefully timed. While lobbying for international recognition for the new Yugoslav Federation and the lifting of sanctions, he was forced to bide his time. Since becoming a participant in the peace process — and with one eye on this autumn's elections — he has moved to patch the holes in the media blanket covering his country.

Elsewhere in the Balkans, independent journalism is faring no better. In 1989, Kosovo lost its media as well as its political autonomy. *Rilindija,* an Albanian-language daily, has been banned and now enters the country from Switzerland where it is sent for printing. Pristina RTV has been put under the supervision of Belgrade RTV, undisputed boss of the Serbian airwaves. Frequencies are no longer allocated to private companies and Kosovo's Albanians are thrown back on receiving Albanian television and radio from Tirana. There are also foreign stations for those with the equipment.

In Montenegro, the old national RTV, some local radio stations, the leading daily *Pobjeda* (Victory), as well as weekly and monthly publications, are tightly controlled by the regime. RTV, local radio and *Pobjeda* are state owned, their management coming exclusively from the ranks of the governing party. Any attempts to shed this supervision, as radio Tivat tried to do, is nipped in the bud. With the notable exception of the weekly *Monitor*, most publications claiming to be independent are organs of various political parties. Montenegro's courts descend swiftly on journalists and proprietors they consider have 'damaged the reputation of the state and its representatives'.

In the Former Yugoslav Republic of Macedonia (FYROM) official television and radio as well as the dailies *Nova Makedonia* and *Vecer* are under government supervision. Some newspapers claim to be independent, but in fact they are tied to one or other of the political parties. The radio and television situation is complex. There are not less than 300 radio stations and 17 private television channels, but they mainly transmit films, shows and programmes from the neighbouring countries, above all from Serb television.

Bosnia-Hercegovina is a special case. No single newspaper, radio or TV station covers the whole country. As new operations are set up, the media map will precisely reflect the country's hardening ethnic divisions: Serb, Croat and Bosnian.

In Croatia, with the exception of the weekly *Drzavnost* (an offshoot of the ruling party's newspaper), none of the 702 radio and TV stations is formally under state supervision. But of the five leading dailies, most of whom were firmly committed to the presidential line during the war, only *Novi List* is making any attempt to move away from state control. Tudjman accuses it of favouring the opposition — 'different anti-Croat movements, not Croat independence' — and the paper has been summoned to pay US$2.5 million tax arrears from which it had been exempted in 1993. Other major Zagreb dailies, like *Vjesnik*, owned by Privredna Banka Zagreb, are regular supporters of government and president.

Around the scattered regions of Croatia the situation varies. The majority shareholders of some papers, Rijeka's *Vecernji List* and *Novi List,* for instance, are journalists. In Osijek, Eastern Slavonia, *Glas Slavonije* is supervised by the local authorities; a new independent daily, *Gradanski List*, financed by a local entrepreneur, is due to open in the new year. Until the advent of its new owner, Miroslav Kutle, a former insurance company clerk, in 1992, *Slobodna Dalmacija*, was considered the most outspoken Croat daily.

The governments of Zagreb and Belgrade treat press freedom in similar cavalier style: economic strangulation, parliamentary pressure and physical violence against journalists who refuse to toe the line. Franjo Tudjman and Slobodan Milosevic are only too aware of the importance of the image transmitted into Croat and Serb homes. The media is no more than a powerful means of collective hypnosis: propaganda. The only independent publications to survive are those with insignificant circulations and little influence; their total circulation cannot begin to compete with the Serbian government-owned daily *Politika*. *Vreme,* the excellent Belgrade daily with a negligible circulation, is a typical example.

In Croatia, ways are found to curtail the circulation of influential uppity papers that get above themselves. In 1992, when the circulation of the popular weekly, *Danas* (Today), peaked at 100,000, it was virtually banned from the news-stands. In 1994, Split's satirical weekly, *Feral Tribune*, a persistent and witty adversary of Tudjman, was taxed with being a pornographic publication. The charge was lifted only a year later by court order. And still *Feral Tribune* manages to get under the president's skin with its hilarious and scurrilous attacks. On 7 May 1996, its editor and a journalist were charged by the Zagreb prosecutor with 'defamation and insults against the President' (see page 22). The criminal law was amended at the end of March to enable such charges, and has already been used against the weekly *Nacional*.

Throughout the region, but above all in Serbia, official newspapers are subsidised and win out over independent publications that have become too expensive for most readers. 'If no-one hears or reads your opinion, you can express it freely,' is how one journalist on the Belgrade's *Nasa Borba* sums it up. And public apathy, developed by decades of a supine media pedalling official propaganda, makes the job of the present regimes that much easier. While the nationalisation of Studio B provoked protests abroad, at home only 200 turned out for the protest demonstration outside RTV's headquarters in Belgrade. ❏

Romana Dobnikar-Seruga writes for Delo, *Ljubljana*

First published in Delo, *Ljubljana*
Translated from the French in Courrier International *by Nicholas McAulay*

MARINKO CULIC

Kingdom for a horse

'Better one thoroughbred president than a field of also-ran opposition'

Croatian President Franjo Tudjman proposes to bring together the bones of victims and their torturers in a 'joint memorial' on the site of their World War II concentration camp. For denouncing this latest 'symbol of reconciliation', Marinko Culic and the editor of **Feral Tribune** were sued for 'defamation of the President'. Their case has been deferred until 25 September

WHY HAS Croatian President Franjo Tudjman chosen this precise moment to launch his 'new reconciliation offensive'? For this is what his announcement on the repatriation of the remains of Tito [currently in Belgrade], Ante Pavelic [pro-Nazi head of the 'Independent State of Croatia' (NDH) in WWII, who died in Madrid in 1959], Vlatko Macek [Croat politician who refused the presidency of the NDH in 1941] and Busic [exiled Croat nationalist killed in Paris by the Yugoslav secret service in 1969] amounts to.

And why does he want to turn the former concentration camp at Jasenovac, where between 100,000 and 150,000 Serbs, Gypsies, Jews and Croat partisans were murdered during the war, into a memorial to all victims? This in spite of warnings from Jewish and official US circles that he should stop his attempts to 'rewrite history with a shovel', and calls from Croatians to desist 'before it is too late'.

To get to the bottom of this 'offensive', one has to remember that in his analysis of the Zagreb crisis Tudjman claimed that if Croatia was to avoid more 'Wiener Neue Stadts, Bleiburgs and Jasenovacs' it must stop the activities of the 'seven-headed coalition' whose aim it was to 'overthrow the only democratically elected authority in Croatia'.

Since it is pointless to talk about the reconciliation of the dead while the living are divided into two camps — those in power and those in opposition — and there is virtually no communication between them, it is obvious that the Croatian leader has no recourse but to introduce 'reconciliation' on to his own party political agenda.

Tudjman is incapable of understanding the roots of the impasse or of finding a way out of it. As a result, he is repeatedly surprised that none of the opposition parties wants to form a coalition with the Croatian Democratic Community (HDZ), while elsewhere in the world parties with 36.5 per cent of the vote have no difficulty finding coalition partners. There is an element of truth in what he says, but what he has failed to understand is that anywhere else in the world, the party in power would examine its own responsibility before accusing other parties. Politically as well as personally, Tudjman is incapable of any such undertaking and he therefore insists on this imposed Franco-style 'reconciliation' rather than a consensual reconciliation of the Adenauer type. His reference to Franco not only confirms his political blindness — if the Spaniards can do without their fascist dictator, what need do Croats have of the like? — it also demonstrates his historical blindness, that is to say, his ignorance of certain fundamental historical facts. Franco's cross of reconciliation, inscribed 'They are present' — all too reminiscent of the Ustashe slogan 'They are with us'— failed to unite republicans and fascists in Spain as Tudjman claims. Reconciliation was the result of the democratic transformation of Spain after Franco's death.

If one wants to borrow anything from Spain, it should be the de-Francoing of the country and not the establishment of a fascist-Communist country led by a two-headed Tudjman, half Tito, half Pavelic

MARINKO CULIK

(the one or the other in the ascendant according to prevailing political circumstances). However, this is evidently just what the Croatian leader wants: it explains his continuous attacks on the opposition who offer in practice the real example of 'reconciliation'. In his own words, it has gathered into its ranks 'everyone from Communists to fascists'.

Why Tudjman should be allowed to reconcile dead fathers when the opposition is not allowed to do the same with their sons, remains unclear. His accusations are a fabrication: even the president can see that the members of the opposition are neither greater Communists nor greater fascists than he himself. The truth of the matter is that he fears opposition leaders like Tomac who have truly accepted the idea of 'reconciliation'; alongside the HDZ, but under a different leadership, another political 'association' is growing.

The evidence that others were proving more successful at reconciliation forced Tudjman to bolster his own party's version by returning Tito's and Pavelic's remains to Croatia and lining them up side by side with their dead armies and followers in Jasenovac. Even if the only problem with transforming Jasenovac was that the bones of the victims would mix with those of their executioners, it would be morbid and crazy enough. But things are worse yet. Tudjman sees his 'new' Jasenovac as 'a reminder to the Croatian people that it was divided in the past and pushed into a fratricidal war'.

Non-Croat victims do not deserve a mention: the aim is to turn a charnel-house where many different nationalities lie into the instrument of internal reconciliation between Croats. Tudjman, meanwhile, clearly neither accepts nor acknowledges when he sees it the true meaning of international reconciliation as symbolised by Brandt kneeling in penance before the monument commemorating the dead of the Warsaw ghetto.

This reconciliatory nightmare into which Tudjman is pushing his 'subjects' has only one incontrovertible result: the more the talk of reconciliation, the deeper the divisions among its supposed participants. While Tudjman is not wholly to blame for the Croat-Serb dispute, he alone is responsible for the conflict between Croats. ❏

Marinko Culic writes for Feral Tribune

Excerpted from Feral Tribune, *Split, Croatia, 4 April 1996*
Translated from the French in Courrier International *by Judith Vidal-Hall*

US DIVIDES

PETER PRINGLE

Albania 1995: exporting the problem

Billboard wars

The battle over tobacco rages on as the industry suppresses information and muzzles criticism

A US$9-AN-HOUR clerk stole internal company documents that exposed the tobacco industry's knowledge of nicotine addiction and threatened its ability to fend off billion-dollar claims. The reaction? The tobacco company in question obtained a court order that forbade the unfortunate clerk from speaking up — even to his own lawyer. On the track of the stolen documents, the company found the papers had been deposited in a university archive in San Francisco, there for all to see. What did the company do? It sent private detectives to harass the archivists and make a list of who had been reading the documents.

In another case, CBS television one day pulled a programme off the air that had a former industry executive talking about how his tobacco company used rat poison in pipe tobacco. Several weeks later, and after much haranguing from media colleagues, CBS aired the programme. In retaliation, the tobacco company released a long dossier on the executive's private life, trying to paint him as an unreliable witness.

The list goes on. But in a recent turn of fate in the tobacco wars, the companies themselves are the ones claiming to have been wronged by having their freedom of speech rights violated.

Invoking First Amendment rights, the companies are trying to fight proposed government bans on billboards displaying the Marlboro cowboy, the cartoon character Joe Camel and a variety of other romantic advertisements of beach scenes and mountain streams that seek to lure the young into the smoking habit.

The Clinton administration, with Hillary at the helm of an anti-tobacco crusade, and several state attorneys-general want billboards that carry such ads taken down if they are within 1,000 feet of a school or a playground. The governments argue that the tobacco companies, experiencing a declining market among adults, have been targeting youth. The figures for teenage smokers are rising. One way that government can execute its public health mandate and help to enforce statutes that forbid the under-18s to buy cigarettes is to prevent the tobacco companies inflicting their subliminal messages on unprotected audiences.

Few things are more American than billboards, and the tobacco companies have reacted with the fervour of a persecuted religious sect. For one thing, the companies claim they don't target youth. None of their romantic cigarette ads, nor their little promotional trinkets, duly stamped Marlboro, or Camel, or Virginia Slims, or whatever, have any 'proven' connection to youth smoking, the companies say. Indeed, they claim that these ads do not induce people to start smoking; they only direct people to buy certain brands. They refer their critics to Aristotle: the word 'dog' never bit anyone.

Almost everyone, except the tobacco companies and their allies, believes that cigarette advertising at least assists the process of a youth deciding to take up smoking. But, shamelessly, the tobacco companies claim the limited protection afforded under the First Amendment to so-called 'commercial speech'. The companies argue that the protection covers cigarette ads just like soap ads — never mind that almost half a million Americans die each year from tobacco-related diseases.

Actually, the Supreme Court protection of advertising is relatively recent, and is constantly under review. The Justices first accepted the idea of commercial free speech in 1976, but they pointedly refused to equate commercial advertising with the inalienable right of the lone political or religious dissenter to preach his views on the street corner — the original intention of the First Amendment. And the ruling specifically recognised that 'child pornography and cigarette advertising' will never be fully protected by the First Amendment.

Later the Court added, '[We] have afforded commercial speech a limited measure of protection, commensurate with its subordinate position in the scale of First Amendment values...'

THE FIRST shots in the tobacco billboard war were fired in Harlem, in 1990. The Rev Calvin Butts led his Abyssinian Baptist congregation in protests against tobacco and alcohol ads that plastered their poor neighbourhoods. He started a nationwide movement that now includes several states and cities. The latest is Cincinnati, Ohio, which banned tobacco billboard ads near schools and playgrounds.

The biggest battle of the billboards has been fought in Baltimore, where the progressive public health and education efforts of the city's black mayor Ed Schmoke inevitably turned on tobacco and alcohol. Baltimore was sued by a billboard company, opposing the ban. The city won in the lower and the appeal court, and the case is now before the Supreme Court.

The key legal test on billboard advertising comes from a case in New York's Hudson River valley where the local electric company had contested a state law designed to encourage fuel conservation by prohibiting electric utilities from advertising electrical appliances. In ruling in favour of the electric company, the Court set a four-part test for such government-imposed restrictions: is the advertising promoting an illegal or misleading product; is the government's interest in regulating the advertising 'substantial'; will that government interest be 'directly advanced' by the restriction, and is the restriction 'more extensive than necessary to serve that interest'?

Baltimore did not attempt to claim that cigarette advertising was misleading — although it certainly could have done. The city did maintain, however, that it had a 'substantial' interest in the billboard ban because of its responsibilities in keeping minors from smoking. About 3,000 teenagers start smoking every day in the US and nearly one billion packs of cigarettes are sold to minors. As 1.5 million adult smokers quit each year, and another 430,000 die of tobacco-related diseases, tobacco commerce relies on the youth market for survival. The city wanted to do what it could to cut down the numbers of smokers.

Baltimore also argued that as the tobacco companies spend about US$6 billion year promoting and advertising their products they must gain from such an outlay. Despite what the tobacco companies say about their ads only affecting brand choice, the courts have routinely recognised a connection between advertising and overall demand for a product. Thus, Baltimore asserted, the government interest would be 'directly advanced' by a billboard ban.

Finally, Baltimore claimed that the billboard ban was not 'more extensive than necessary' because other media were left untouched. The tobacco companies could still advertise in newspapers, magazines and direct mail. Magazines carry about 60 per cent of the US$440 million spent annually by the tobacco companies on print and outdoor advertising.

The appeals court agreed that Baltimore's ban was not 'excessive' — upholding a Supreme Court ruling of 60 years ago that allowed the Mormon state of Utah to keep its complete ban on all outdoor smoking and alcohol ads. The ruling said that '... Advertisements of this sort are constantly before the eyes of the observers on streets and in street cars to be seen without the exercise of choice or volition on their part...the young people as well as adults have the message of the billboard thrust upon them with all the arts and devices that skill can produce.'

Earlier this year, the Supreme Court ruled again on 'commercial speech'. The tiny state of Rhode Island has a 40-year-old law banning the advertising of liquor prices. The idea is that by discouraging bargain-hunting and keeping liquor prices high the state will, in effect, be discouraging liquor consumption. There are similar bans in Connecticut, Pennsylvania and eight other states.

The Rhode Island case started in 1991 when a liquor store owner placed ads in a newspaper that tried to circumvent the price ban. Next to bottles of vodka and rum was the word 'WOW' in large letters. Judging this to be tantamount to a price ad, the state fined the store US$400, whereupon the store sued the state. The case went to the Supreme Court which invalidated the state ban on mentioning prices, saying the state had violated the First Amendment's guarantee of free speech.

In the Court's main opinion, Justice John Paul Stevens said the ban was illegal because it prevented people from having access to information to which they should be entitled. 'The First Amendment', he wrote, 'directs us to be especially sceptical of regulations that keep people in the dark for what the government perceives to be their own good.' Noting that advertising had been 'a part of our culture throughout our history', he added that in limiting product advertising regulators must consider alternatives that do not interfere with free speech. Instead, government should more strictly control the use of the product itself, he said. In other words, restricting speech is constitutionally more dangerous than restricting the harmful activity which a product allows.

Quite where government and the tobacco companies go from here is not clear. President Clinton, through the Food and Drug Administration, is pressing ahead with its plan to restrict all tobacco advertising 'that reaches children', including billboards and retail outlets. The tobacco companies are challenging those rules in court.

The political and legal siege of Big Tobacco has become so intense that there are signs of a crack in the companies' armour. The US$45 billion industry has been putting out feelers for a deal: remove the hounds of government regulation and we will behave more appropriately towards youth, say the companies.

In May, the market leader, Philip Morris, with its runaway Marlboro brand, proposed a ban on cigarette vending machines, which represent one of the key sources of tobacco for minors. Philip Morris also proposed a reduction of promotional trinkets that attract youth to cigarettes — and restrictions on billboard advertising; the very intrusion that the company had been challenging so vigorously on First Amendment grounds.

The other big tobacco enterprises have yet to join Philip Morris in this pipe of peace. An advertising ban would give them a reduced opportunity to challenge the market leader. For the moment, the offer can hardly be taken as genuine. ❏

Peter Pringle is a journalist based in New York. He is currently writing a book on the tobacco industry

OPINION

NASR ABU ZAID

THE POLITICS of the interpretation of the Quran lie at the heart of the Abu Zaid case. In the eyes of orthodox Islam, the Quran is the eternal word of God. As it always existed, it was never created. That this eternal text should have been revealed to the Prophet Mohammed in seventh-century Arabia has no bearing on the meaning of the Quran, which is a book to be read literally and holds true for all times. Consequently there is no tradition of textual criticism of the Quran analogous to those for the Hebrew Bible and New Testament.

THE INDEPENDENT/DAVID ROSE

The case of Abu Zaid

However, this orthodox view has been challenged by Islamic scholars over the centuries. A rationalist school emerged in the ninth century under the Abbasid Empire, known as the Mu'tazilites, whose doctrines fused notions of social justice with a purified, spiritualised monotheism. They argued for a created Quran by distinguishing between God's essence, which they held to be eternal and beyond human understanding, and His word, which is created and accessible to reason.

While the Mu'tazilites were marginalised after two decades, their thought remained influential down to the present, as evinced in the writings of Abu Zaid himself. Here he sets out the evolution of his scholarship from the beginning of his *career as a graduate student to his most recent scholarly works. Abu Zaid has applied contemporary methods of textual criticism to his study of the Quran, contextualising the book in its historical setting. This challenge to orthodoxy, he argues, has been used as a pretext by those who perhaps had more personal reasons to seek his downfall.*

THERE are many aspects to the story of Abu Zaid.

Let us take first the academic aspect. This covers the need to raise new questions if knowledge in any given field is to be advanced.

A second aspect concerns the political implications of such scholarship when the subject matter in question is a religion, namely Islam, frequently subjected to political manipulation during its long history. Given the present social and political state of the entire Muslim world, and the plethora of Islamist political movements, any critical approach to Islamic thought is condemned and the life of its perpetrator endangered.

The third and last aspect is a personal one. This will not be explored here.

ABU ZAID began his career as an assistant teacher in the department of Arabic, Faculty of Letters, Cairo University, immediately after graduation in 1972. Though highly unusual, the department committee decided that the newly appointed assistant should take 'Islamic Studies' as his major field of research in both his Masters and PhD theses. The faculty committee approved the decision.

It is important at this point to record that the decision in question was intended to convince Abu Zaid, himself reluctant to major in this subject, that the need for a specialist in Islamic studies was most urgent. Abu Zaid's reluctance was based on the rejection of a PhD thesis on Islamic studies presented to the department 25 years earlier by Muhammad Ahmad Khalafallah. At the time, Khalafallah was an assistant under the supervision of professor Amin al-Khuly. His thesis, *The Art of Narration in the Quran*, subjects the text to a literary approach formulated by his professor. The university refuted the thesis after a heated debate on the validity of such an approach to the Muslim holy book.

Similar debates followed the publication of Ali Abd al-Razik's *Islam and the Principles of Political Authority* in 1925 and Taha Husayn's *Pre-Islamic Poetry* in 1928.

Following the rejection of his thesis, Khalafallah was transferred to a non-teaching job in the Ministry of Education; his professor was forbidden to teach or supervise Islamic studies. Five years later, in 1954, a government decree forced Amin al-Khuly into retirement along with many other professors. This decision, initiated by the new military authority, ironically called 'The Free Officers Movement', was presented to the public as part of a revolutionary process intended to remove corruption from Egyptian society and to 'cleanse the universities'. The chair of Islamic Studies fell vacant; teaching at the undergraduate level fell to any professor interested in teaching it.

Aware of the consequences that might follow the application of any non-traditional method to Islamic studies, Abu Zaid tried in vain to convey his fears on the risks implicit in majoring in Islamic studies to the department committee. The department countered by stressing the need to appoint a specialist to the long-abandoned chair in Islamic studies for instruction in the subject.

At this point, Abu Zaid gave up his objections and set about examining the different methods of interpretation historically applied to the text of the Quran. Starting with the concept of 'metaphor' introduced to Arabic Rhetoric by the rationalist Mu'tazilite school of theology, Abu Zaid took 'The Concept of Metaphor as Applied to the Quran by the Mu'tazilites' as the subject of his Masters thesis. This was later published as *The Rational Exegesis of the Quran* (first ed Beirut 1982, fourth ed 1996).

After four years of analysing and comparing the discourse of the Mu'tazilites and their critics, Abu Zaid concluded that the Quran was the site of a fierce intellectual and political debate. Battle was joined at one of the most important junctures in the structure of the Quranic text (Chap III v 7): the point at which, unambiguous verses (*ayaat muhkamat*), the backbone of the Book, confront ambiguous verses (*ayat mutashabihaat*), the latter to be interpreted in the light of the former. While the Mu'tazilites and their opponents agree on principle, in practice they part company. The controversy revolves around the meaning of the Quran as well as its structure: what the Mu'tazilites considered 'unambiguous' their opponents considered 'ambiguous' and vice versa.

The intellectual battle was the ultimate expression of a socio-political struggle involving different world views. Seeking an interpretative framework ostensibly devoid of political interests, Abu Zaid chose for his doctoral research to study the hermeneutics of the Quran within a Sufi, or mystical Islamic context.

Accordingly, the subject of Abu Zaid's PhD thesis was *The Hermeneutics of the Quran by Muhiy Al-Deen Ibn Arabi*. Ibn Arabi, a great Andalusian Sufi, was born in Spain and wrote his greatest treatise, *Al-Futuhat Al-Makkiah* (The Meccan Revelation) in Mecca, and died in Syria in 638 H (1279 AD).

In the process, Abu Zaid came to much the same conclusion as before: namely, all interpretation is informed by contemporary socio-political and cultural factors. Ibn Arabi's purpose was to incorporate into Quranic interpretation the advances in knowledge up to and including contemporary developments. He wanted to ensure that Islam was an open-ended faith, one that could reconcile itself to, and indeed incorporated, Christianity, Judaism and all other religions. It was to be the 'religion of comprehensive love' described by Ibn Arabi in his poetry. His methodology was very much a product of contemporary Andalusian society based on its linguistic, cultural and ethnic pluralism: Provençale was spoken in the streets, Latin in the Church, classical Arabic in the court and a multitude of local dialects elsewhere. Ibn Arabi sought to reconcile all elements and groups.

Needless to say, the project failed. Ibn Arabi's attempt to construct a personal utopia was driven by the increasing tension and conflict within his society. Abu Zaid's thesis on Ibn Arabi was published as *The Philosophy of Hermeneutics* (first ed Beirut 1983, third ed 1996).

As an Egyptian, Abu Zaid witnessed a similar conflict over the meaning of Islam in contemporary religious discourse, particularly the rival interpretations of Islam in the 1960s and 1970s. In the 1960s, the dominant religious discourse presented Islam as the religion of social justice, urging its followers to fight imperialism and Zionism. In the 1970s, with the open-door economic policy and the peace with Israel, Islam became the religion that guarded private property and urged Muslims to make peace with the Israelis.

The chances of ever escaping the impasse created by this pragmatic exegesis of the Quran began to exercise Abu Zaid. And even if it were practically feasible, how could it be done? Being by now acutely aware that the interpretation of the Quran is not and has never been an innocent pursuit devoid of socio-political and cultural impact; and that at times it goes even further and becomes deliberate political manipulation of the text, Abu Zaid nevertheless put the 'Concept of the Text' back at the centre of his academic research.

The result of this research was a third book, *Mafhum Al-Nass: Dirasah fi Ulum Al-Quran* (The Concept of the Text: A Study of the Sciences of the Quran), first published in Cairo in 1990 with many subsequent editions in Beirut and Casablanca. It proposed that before dealing with questions of interpretation, one must first define the nature of the text and, since the way should not be left open for any and every interpretation, examine the rules governing the study of that text.

The study of modern hermeneutics had revealed to Abu Zaid the dangers of leaving a religious text prey to interpretation by all and sundry. Religious texts, especially in Islam, profoundly influence social and cultural life. Scholars of religious texts have to set out the limits of certainty and the interpretative scope of such texts if they are not to be reduced to vehicles for competing ideologies. And, in the process, religion may be perverted from its true purpose: the good of humanity in this world and the next.

No text comes free of historical context. As text, the Quran is no exception and is, therefore, a proper subject for interpretation. Indeed, throughout its history, the Quran has been the subject of various schools of interpretation. Abu Zaid set out to investigate these within their historical context.

To say that the Quran is an historical text in no way implies that its origins are human. However, given that God's eternal word was revealed to Mohammed in seventh-century Arabia at a specific time and place, this makes it an historical text. Whereas God's eternal word exists in a sphere beyond human knowledge, an historical text may be subject to historical interpretation and understanding. Just as the Mu'tazilites, Ash'araites, Shi'ites and Sufis historically used their different methods of interpretation to serve particular socio-political ends, so it could be demonstrated that contemporary religio-political discourse was doing precisely the same.

Abu Zaid, scholar and citizen, dreaming of a better future for his country and its people, as well as progress within the Islamic world, felt himself under a compulsion to examine modern Islamic discourse. His critical analysis was published as *Naqd Al-Khitab Al-Diny* (Critique of Islamic Discourse) in Cairo in 1992, with a third edition in 1996. This was the book that began all Abu Zaid's troubles.

Muftis in the making: Fouad 1st Islamic Institute run by Al-Azhar

IN MAY 1992, Abu Zaid applied to the department of Arabic studies for promotion to full professor. His previous five years' academic output, 11 papers and two books, was submitted to an advisory committee responsible for evaluating the level of scholarship and forwarding a report with its recommendations to the dean of the faculty. Departmental professors are also given copies of the report informing them of the committee's decision and inviting comment.

It took the committee almost seven months — rather than the statutory three — to reach its decision. It was 3 December before departmental professors finally received its recommendation to reject Abu Zaid's promotion.

Meanwhile, word had got out that far from being the unanimous verdict claimed in the report itself, the rejection had got through by the narrowest of margins: seven against, six in favour. Furthermore, it came out that of the three experts consulted by the committee, two declared strongly in Abu Zaid's favour. However, and despite the protest of certain committee members who refused to endorse the report, the minority opinion prevailed.

The decision of the committee, as for much that followed, was the result of social and political pressures from outside. Only the fear that characterises any discussion of religious matters [in Egypt] explains the farce that went on inside the committee that resulted in the majority being terrorised into silence by one voice.

Yet we should be remiss if we did not also note the personal animosity that crept in to what should have been an objective, scholarly assessment of Abu Zaid's work. For one committee member, Dr Abd el-Sabour Shahin, personal revenge clouded academic judgement to the point where he not only voted against Abu Zaid's appointment, he had him labelled an apostate.

The trouble began with the introductory pages to *Critique of Islamic Discourse* in which the author criticises the so-called 'Islamic investment companies' that had been set up as alternatives to the usurious and un-Islamic practices of the modern, western banking sector.

Now it happened that Shahin, the dissenting voice among the Islamic experts consulted by the committee, was also the religious advisor to one of these 'Islamic' institutions that had featured at the centre of a great public scandal in 1988. With his own reputation at stake, it would seem that Shahin attempted to save his own skin by using what should have been a purely academic report on Abu Zaid's scholarship to discredit his authority as a Muslim by labelling him an apostate.

According to Abu Zaid, it was only the endorsement of exponents of 'political Islam' like Shahin, in company with prominent representatives of orthodox Islam led by the rector of Al-Azhar, the late Gad Al-Haqu 'Ali Gad Al-Haqu, that enabled these institutions successfully to carry out the biggest financial swindle in modern Egyptian banking history. Trusting in these experts and their exploitation of Islam, hundreds of thousands of Egyptians lost their entire savings. While the former were busy attacking the interest rates charged by the modern banking system, there was a good deal of self-interest at work in the rival Islamic companies.

Abu Zaid's introductory observations were to Shahin as a red rag to a bull. His 'academic' report neither took account of the remaining chapters of *Critique of Islamic Discourse*, nor its methodology. Once they had seen the report, the department professors rose up in protest. In a letter to the dean supporting Abu Zaid's promotion, they objected to the contents as well as the tenor of the report. Shahin, they argued, had neither kept abreast of scholarly research, nor familiarised himself with theoretical developments such as semiotics. Moreover, he had either not read — or failed to appreciate — Abu Zaid's full body of work. The departmental committee also agreed, unanimously, that in failing to carry out an objective, scholarly evaluation and taking up matters of dogma, Shahin's report exceeded the scope of the promotion committee's brief 'to investigate exclusively the scholarly production without concern for any other consideration'. As was evident from its language, the report was passing judgement on Abu Zaid's faith rather than his academic credentials.

Academically, matters came to a head when all the documents in the case of Abu Zaid — the report of the academic committee rejecting the appointment, the departmental opinion in Abu Zaid's favour and the faculty committee's endorsement of this — were presented for a final decision to the rector of Cairo University.

Once again, intellectual terrorism prevailed over justice. Anxious at all costs to avoid either a stand off with the Islamists, or offending the government on whom his job — like all state university rectors — depended, and which, at the time, was taking a soft line on Islamist terrorism, Dr Ma'mun Salama chose to regard the affair as an everyday case of a failed academic promotion rather than as a threat to academic values and freedoms. Easier — and safer too for all concerned, he judged — to advise Abu Zaid quietly to 'try again later' when he could be sure of promotion, than to risk a confrontation with the Islamists in the university or jeopardise the government's attempt at compromise with them.

Dr Salama could not have been more wrong. Abu Zaid was not saved from the wrath of the Islamists; academic freedom and the reputation of Cairo University suffered a serious setback. Only two weeks after the university's decision not to confer a full professorship on Abu Zaid, Shahin used the pulpit of a central Cairo mosque, Amr Ibn Al-Aas mosque, publicly to proclaim Abu Zaid an apostate. That was on Friday 2 April 1993. The following Friday, mosques throughout Egypt followed suit. These even included the small mosque in Abu Zaid's home village, close to the city of Tanta, capital of the Delta, whose preacher had grown up and gone to the same *kuttab* — traditional Quranic school — as Abu Zaid where they had learned and memorised the Quran together. For him, as for so many others, Shahin was a reliable authority, beyond question. Had not the university itself added to his credibility by endorsing his verdict?

It needed only one person, it seems, to lead a venomous campaign not only against an individual called Abu Zaid, but against the entire intellectual tradition presented in his work. Even so, things could not have taken the course they did, had we not reached a point at which certain individuals are treated as sacrosanct: men protected by God himself, against error and above the law. There are those whose understanding and exposition of religion enjoys a near sacred authority simply because they stick to time-worn views, never questioning but repeating endlessly what has been said for centuries. Given this intellectual stagnation, it is easy to brand any breath of fresh air in the form of new explanations or interpretations of religion as blasphemous. Proof of apostasy needs only the demonstration that non-traditional methods of investigation have been used.

Once Abu Zaid's apostasy had been trumpeted from the pulpit, the next step was to prove it in court. The plot to do this was hatched in a mosque in the Pyramids neighbourhood. Its preacher, a teacher with Shahin at Dar al-Ulum, and one of his followers, proposed to take the issue to the Family Court. He argued that the marriage of Abu Zaid to his wife Dr Ebtehal Yunes, an associate professor of French civilisation in her husband's faculty at the university, should be annulled on the grounds that Islamic law forbids the marriage of an apostate to a Muslim. In a book distributed free inside the university to Abu Zaid's students, Shahin's disciple writes that he consulted the dean of Dar al-Ulum and a former minister of culture, now a professor, about his lawsuit. Once their blessing was secured, Islamist lawyers volunteered their services and funds were collected to cover other expenses.

Abu Zaid's opponents made it clear from the outset that the marital status of Abu Zaid was of less concern than getting his apostasy legally confirmed by the state. To do so, they took advantage of a loophole in the Family Code, otherwise integrated within the Secular Egyptian Civil Code, to introduce cases in Islamic personal status law or *hisbah*. On the precedent of a centuries-old Islamic ruling that disallows the marriage of a Muslim to a non-Muslim, a group of Islamist lawyers petitioned for the divorce of Abu Zaid from Ebtehal Yunes (*Index* 7/1993). Such a ruling would confirm Abu Zaid's status as an apostate and allow his opponents to press for his dismissal from the university.

On 15 April 1993, the supposedly 'moderate' Islamic weekly *Al-Liwa' al-Islami*, founded by the ruling National Democratic Party to counter religious extremism and terrorism, ran an editorial fulminating against the 'heretic' Abu Zaid who had endangered the faith of his students and urging the rector of the university to fire him. A week later, the same paper counselled the government that 'execution' was the only fitting penalty for Abu Zaid — and that it should apply the provisions of the Islamic penal code immediately. On top of this came the pronouncement from Sheikh Mohammed el-Ghazali, a leading authority among Islamists, during the trial of the assassins of Farag Fouda (*Index* 7/1992 & 7/1993): if the state did not do its religious duty, he opined, it was the duty of every Muslim to execute the punishment. The covert aim of the Islamists was to have Abu Zaid legally killed in the name of Islam. On 27 January 1994, the judge in the First Grade Family Court ruled the case inadmissible because the plaintiff had insufficient personal grievance with Abu Zaid. The decision was challenged in the court of appeal and overturned. The Islamists succeeded in having Abu Zaid's apostasy confirmed and his marriage officially annulled.

Abu Zaid took his case to the Court of Cassation, Egypt's final court of appeal. The case is now in court. There is no recourse beyond its decision.

His case generated widespread public protest and attracted media and human rights interest worldwide.

Meanwhile, the price Abu Zaid and Ebtehal Yunes have paid for taking on their enemies in court and opposing any manipulation of Islam, is flight from Egypt and all that entails: the loss of country, home, students and colleagues. ❏

INTERVIEW

MOHAMMED SAYED TANTAWI

MIDDLE EAST TIMES

Time for change

After 10 years as Egyptian state mufti, Mohammed Sayed Tantawi was appointed Grand Sheikh of Al-Azhar mosque on 27 March. During his tenure as mufti, Tantawi, 68, advanced a liberal interpretation of Islam that was applauded by some but opposed by others, mainly conservative scholars at the 1,000-year-old Al-Azhar. In the following interview with Amira Howeldy of Al Ahram, *Sheikh Tantawi spells out his position on a number of controversial issues. Commentators, including Nasr Abu Zaid, are optimistic that his appointment to the country's most influential Islamic institution may ameliorate some of its more pressing problems*

Following your appointment as sheikh of Al-Azhar, you were quoted as saying that you would feel able to retract some of your previous fatwas *[religious rulings], provided you were shown evidence from the Quran and the* Sunna *[the Prophet Mohammed's teachings] that was stronger than the evidence you already had. Were you referring to any* fatwas *in particular?*

NO. This is a general ruling. A true Muslim should not be stubborn, but should follow the truth once he establishes that it is the truth.

Our master, God's Prophet, provided us with a good example. He would order his companions to do certain things or refrain from doing certain things because it was necessary given the circumstances at the time. But once circumstances changed, the order would be dropped.

But in a recent press interview, you condoned female genital mutilation, although you had stated previously that the religious texts favouring this practice were too weak.

I still stand by the official *fatwa* published in the twenty-third volume of *fatwas* passed by Dar El-Efta'a [the mufti's office], in which I stated clearly that female genital mutilation is a custom that has nothing to do with worship. All the *hadiths* [Prophet's sayings] that deal with female genital mutilation are weakly sourced and should not be relied upon.

This is not just my opinion, but also that of other imams, such as Imam El-Shawkani and Sheikh Sayed Sabeq, who discussed the matter in his book, *Sunni Jurisprudence.*

You are also said to have changed your position on visiting Jerusalem. While you were previously reported as being willing to visit the city if invited by Yasser Arafat, more recent reports quote you as saying that you would not visit Jerusalem until its liberation. What is your position?

I still say that if I receive an invitation from President Yasser Arafat to visit Jerusalem and offer prayers at Al-Aqsa mosque, I will welcome this invitation, as long as the conditions allow it.

Are these conditions related to the liberation of Jerusalem?

No: we are talking from a religious, not a political, perspective.

Do you agree with the statement issued by Al-Azhar Ulama [Islamic scholars] Committee describing the suicide bombers who killed Israeli civilians as 'the best of martyrs' because Israel is a Dar Harb [battlefield]?

No. Anybody who blows himself up on a battlefield to defend his religion, his country or his honour is a martyr. But I cannot equate a man who blows himself up to kill enemies who have declared war on Islam with someone who blows himself up, killing children, women, Muslims and non-Muslims in the process. My words on this are as clear as the sun.

The Ulama's statement was interpreted as marking the beginning of dissension within Al-Azhar.

Everybody has the right to speak his mind. We don't gag people. But I repeat that I cannot equate someone who blows himself up to kill enemies who have declared war on us with someone who blows himself up to kill Muslims, non–Muslims, children and women.

The Holy Quran exhorts us to 'fight, in God's cause, those who fight you'. Please emphasise the words 'those who fight you'. It also exhorts us 'not to commit aggression because God does not love the aggressors'.

You have previously stated that the interest of the nation is determined by the political authorities. To what extent are your fatwas linked to those authorities?

By the nation's interest, I mean its political and social interest. When it comes to religious interest, the word of scholars and theologians comes first.

You stated in the past that Dar El-Efta'a should be the sole authority issuing fatwas. Is this position related to the apparent contradiction between some fatwas issued by Dar El-Efta'a and others issued by Al-Azhar over the past few years?

The only body officially authorised to issue *fatwas* in Egypt is Dar El-Efta'a, which is over 100 years old. But this should not prevent any scholar from issuing *fatwas* within the limits of his specialisation and knowledge, and provided he bears responsibility for what he says.

Is this view related to your past experience as mufti?

No, this has nothing to do with being mufti or a professor at Al-Azhar University. I am for truth and for allowing each person his due, and against grabbing [the authority of others]. With all sincerity, I say that the mufti's word regarding what is *halal* [religiously acceptable] and what is *haram* [sinful] comes ahead of the word of the sheikh of Al-Azhar. But when it comes to Azharite institutions, the word of the sheikh of Al-Azhar comes ahead of the mufti's word. And the word of the minister of *Al-Awqaf* [religious endowments] concerning *Al-Da'wa* [propagation of Islam] comes ahead of the words of both the mufti and the sheikh of Al-Azhar.

So what will be the fate of Al-Azhar's Fatwa Committee?

The Fatwa Committee will continue to issue *fatwas*. If these *fatwas* are correct, we will support them, but if they are not, we will urge it to reconsider. The same applies to Dar El-Efta'a. But I repeat, Dar El-Efta'a is the only official body authorised to issue *fatwas*.

Shortly before your new appointment, you were quoted as saying that the trial of Dr Nasr Hamed Abu Zaid should not be conducted in his absence, but that he should be summoned for a discussion of his ideas. Is this true?

What you have just said is 100 per cent untrue. I have never addressed the issue of Nasr Hamed Abu Zaid in any way. It is the custom of theologians, Dar El-Efta'a and Al-Azhar not to comment on cases that are being considered by the judiciary, leaving the courts to have their say. It is only when the judiciary requests the opinion of the mufti or the sheikh of Al-Azhar that he must provide it.

Does this mean the judiciary did not seek your opinion in the case of Abu Zaid?

If the judiciary refers a matter of jurisprudence to us we are under an obligation to respond.

Should we expect major changes at Al-Azhar following your appointment?

Life is a continual process of development. Thanks be to God, Al-Azhar is now over 1,000 years old and, thanks be to God, it has never ceased to develop. If I and the brothers who co-operate with me find that some of the curricula or administrative regulations need to be modified to serve religion, knowledge and the public interest, then we shall make those modifications. But I did not come to Al-Azhar intending to make changes. If I and my brothers find something needs to be changed, we shall change it; if we decide other things should be retained, we shall retain them.

According to the 1961 law governing Al-Azhar, the curricula of Al-Azhar's educational institutes should be reviewed every four years, but this has never been done. Will it be done now?

I am devoting a great deal of attention to this. Books that are included in the curricula in the primary, preparatory and secondary stages will be scrutinised meticulously by me and by specialised committees. What needs to be developed will be developed, what needs to be modified will be modified, what should remain unchanged will remain unchanged. ❑

© *First published in* Al Ahram, *April 1996*

Saudi souvenir: pilgrim poses in photographer's studio, Mecca

The sands run out

On 25 June, in the wake of the 31 May execution of the
six Saudis accused of the November bomb attack on the
National Guard headquarters in Riyadh, a massive bomb
ripped into the multinational base near Dhahran killing
19 US servicemen and wounding many more. Weeks
before, the Saudi rulers had been warned of the violence
to come if US troops remained on the holy land of Islam.
While the White House announced it had no intention of
reducing its presence in the region, wiser counsels in
Washington admitted that this latest manifestation of
domestic unrest had seriously damaged the standing of
Saudi Arabia as 'an island of stability in the region',
confirming the view of our contributors that continuing
repression will lead to further violence

File on Saudi Arabia compiled by Judith Vidal-Hall

ALAIN GRESH

End of an era

The Gulf War was a watershed in Saudi Arabia. Once there was oil, untold wealth, silence and repression. Today, depleted coffers no longer buy silence or compliance. Repression has deepened; domestic unrest is growing. And, from exile, a persistent and vociferous Islamic opposition is aggravating the twin crises of legitimacy and succession afflicting the ruling family

THE CAMERA pans across the crowd, pausing only on the faces of the plainclothes police. The images, in black and white, are fuzzy; the hand-held camera unsteady. The shots seem old-fashioned, reminiscent of snaps smuggled past the censor and customs officers. 'We could be anywhere,' says the voice-over, 'in Pinochet's Chile or Burma under military rule.' But the men gathered here are in floor-length white robes and chequered head-dresses held in place with the *egal*, a silken cord, usually black. Women are invisible.

This is Saudi Arabia, birthplace of Islam and site of one quarter of the world's total oil reserves. For the first time, a militant has been able to film an opposition demonstration in a country from which one is accustomed to hear only the stifled sounds of revolt once these have been snuffed out.

It is 10 September 1994, towards the end of the day. Hundreds of cars escort Sheikh Salman al-Awdah back to the capital, Riyadh, to protect him from arrest or 'disappearance'. The motorcade leads him through Burayda, a town of 100,000 and capital of Qasim province. The next day, his house is surrounded by police; but many of his followers are on guard. They accompany the young sheikh — he is still in his 30s — when he is summoned, in vain, to the governor's residence to renounce his activities. On 13 September the film shows him at the mosque addressing a tightly packed gathering of men. The sheikh recites the words of a Saudi poet:

'They have forbidden the word, writing and speech!
Be silent! And if injustice remains
When the tongue is mute, it will burn like a moth in the flame.
For opinion now is trash, secreted away and thrown in the bin.
The word is a crime,
Beware he who would start a debate.'*

At dawn the following day, the police arrest and imprison the sheikh along with dozens of his followers. The camera tracks the demonstrators as they spread out across the town. Over the next few weeks, the confrontations continue, particularly around the mosques. Two years after the 'uprising of Burayda', Sheikh al-Awdah is still behind bars. The monarchy had decided to strike out against the Islamist dissent that was continuing to gain ground.

In September 1992, 107 prominent members of the community addressed a private memorandum of 45 pages to Sheikh Abdelaziz Bin Baz, the Kingdom's highest religious official. Though they were careful not to attack the king personally, the signatories put forward some revolutionary demands: equality for all before the law, official accountability, an end to corruption and usury, the redistribution of wealth, the strengthening of the army and national independence, the curtailing of police powers. These demands were combined with others of a more militant Islamist nature: more religious courses in the universities, a ban on the teaching of 'western doctrines', censorship of television and foreign programmes and so forth.

It is the origins of the signatories, more than their demands, that worried the authorities: 72 per cent are from the Nadj region; half of them are clerics. Since its foundation, the stability of the Kingdom has been underpinned by the alliance between the family of Al-Saud — whose tribal base is in Najd — and the *ulama* (the guardians of Islamic doctrine), chiefly those descended from Mohammed Ibn Abdel Wahhab, founder of Saudi Arabia's puritanical interpretation of Islam.

In the 1950s and 1960s, opposition movements based on socialism or Arab nationalism gathered support mainly among the Shia minority in the

---

* *'They have forbidden the word' by Abdallah Hamid al-Hamid, assistant lecturer at the University of Riyadh. He was arrested and released in 1993 only 'after having committed himself to withdraw from all political activity considered hostile to the Kingdom'. (AI)*

Eastern Province or in the outlying areas of the country. Relying on the loyalty of the Nadj and armed with the banner of Islam endorsed by the *ulama*, the monarchy was able to defeat them. Today, it is from the heartlands of the Nadj and from the *ulama* itself, speaking in the name of a 'purified' Islam, that the most serious threat comes.

In 1993, confrontation went public. In May of that year, in a country where all political activity is banned, six prominent religious and intellectual figures launched an unprecedented challenge to King Fahd by announcing the formation of the Committee for the Defense of Legitimate Rights (CDLR). It proposed to 'abolish injustice, support the oppressed and defend the rights which have been given to man by the *sharia*'. Their action, they went on to explain was dictated by the desire to 'stop the accelerating deterioration pushing society towards chaos. The only alternative to violence is a balanced and moderate reform movement.'

Their professed moderation did nothing to mitigate royal outrage. In the days that followed, organisers were dismissed from their jobs in the public sector, interrogated and arrested. Some months later, CDLR spokesman Mohammed al-Mas'ari secretly crossed into Yemen en route for London from where he bombards the Kingdom by fax and Internet (see *Index* 3/1996 p9).

'The level of education in Arabia has risen, illiteracy has fallen below 35 per cent, lower than in Egypt. In every home there is someone who knows how to read; everyone has a radio and listens to foreign stations; they can even distinguish between the BBC which they consider biased, and the more objective broadcasts of Dutch radio. The law prohibiting satellite dishes is not being applied and there are between 100,000 and 600,000. Who can stem the tide of information?' Mas'ari reasonably asks.

For Saudi society, the Gulf War was an irreparable trauma. The presence of 500,000 foreign troops on the 'Holy Land of Islam', the inability of the Kingdom to defend itself despite the billions spent on sophisticated weaponry and the systematic destruction of Iraq by the allied armies, provoked questions from a highly nationalistic — not to say xenophobic — and religious population.

Society was run in an archaic, though, from a government perspective, effective manner. The all-powerful, non-elective Council of Princes, representing the most powerful members of the royal family and the major tribes, became the means of communicating to the public only that information the council chose to divulge and of filtering out information

Gulf War trauma: French forces in the desert, 1990

deemed too sensitive for public consumption.

For a long time, recalls another dissident, Khalid al-Fawwaz, director of the Advice and Reformation Committee, a more radical opposition group than the CDLR, people who wanted to change their situation were thrown back on their own resources. 'In the 70s it was difficult to organise collectively,' says al-Fawwaz. 'Officials, even the king, held their weekly public meetings at which they listened to individual grievances — and made promises.' Usuma Bin Ladin, another director of the ARC, was stripped of his citizenship in February 1994 for his financial support of militant Islamic groups in Egypt and elsewhere.

Dissent is by no means limited to the Islamists. Early February 1991 saw the publication of an open letter to King Fahd from 43 liberal businessmen and intellectuals. Their demands, formulated with great deference, were moderate in the extreme: without questioning the *sharia*-based constitution or the monarchy, they called for the creation of consultative councils at the national, provincial and local level, a 'basic law of government' and control over the *Mutaww'in*, the 'morals police'. These demands, including one reference to human rights, were considerably milder than those made by the same liberal opposition in the early 1980s and represented no challenge to the monarchy.

However, in March 1992, the liberals got some satisfaction when the king issued a Basic Law and announced the formation of a Consultative Council and the role to be played by the regions. In August 1993, the king appointed the 60 members of the *majlis*. They were largely made up of 'modern' elites with only nominal representation of the traditional *ulama*. In practical terms, the Consultative Council did nothing to curb the power of the royal family nor increase representation in government. It was more a matter of the king co-opting western-educated Saudis, including certain opponents, who represented little threat to the status quo and could be enlisted against the more dangerous Islamist opposition.

THOUGH excluded from government, the local bourgeoisie has total freedom when it comes to commerce and banking. Weak and wholly dependent on the largesse of the *rentier* state and royal family, they do not constitute a class able or likely to demand any substantial change in the system. On the contrary, they are strongly opposed to an accelerated pace of development.

But since the oil boom of 1973, Saudi society has been convulsed by structural changes that have shaken the traditional power centres. In 1970, 26 per cent of the population lived in cities; in 1990 it was 73 per cent. At the beginning of the 1980s, infant mortality was 118 per 1,000; by 1990 it had fallen to 21 per 1,000. In 1960, only two per cent of girls attended school, but by 1981 this had risen to 41 per cent and, by 1991, was over 80 per cent. Women now make up the majority of graduates — though they are excluded from certain fields like engineering, journalism and architecture for example — but the regular labour market remains virtually closed to them. Their confinement to the family and exclusion from the public arena, especially in the Najd region, is unparalleled in the Muslim world (see page 80).

Young people, more urbanised, better educated and with higher expectations than their parents and less subject to tribal relationships, have also been cut off from their roots. They believed they would be better off than their parents: that the Kingdom's wealth would ensure an easy life. Manual labour was handled by Arab and Asian migrants; even students from modest families aspired to well-paying jobs in the higher ranks of the bloated public sector. The high increase in the number of students, boosted by a birth rate that is among the highest in the world, has been accompanied by a noticeable drop in standards and the appearance of a lumpen graduate class without real qualifications. The development of Islamic universities in the 1970s led to the entry of thousands of new *ulama* on to the market for religious experts, and left them exposed to new currents in a highly charged Muslim world.

By 1986, persistently lower oil revenues left the state — the country's main employer — unable any longer to guarantee employment to all graduates. In 1994, the International Monetary Fund (IMF) predicted that without structural reforms the current deficit would continue to grow to the point where government debt would reach 77 per cent of the gross national product by 1998.

The government faces structural problems that budget tinkering will not solve. And since any obvious remedies threaten to be politically explosive, they are unlikely to take place under the present regime. The introduction of income tax is ruled out for fear that this might lead to demands for political representation, and there is little scope for further cuts in expenditure without running the risk of domestic repercussions (see page 55).

Public sector salaries are a permanent drain on resources. In 1994, these accounted for 51 per cent of expenditure and 90 per cent of oil revenue. Interest payments on domestic debt now account for 10 per cent of state expenditure. Both are likely to grow. Given that the government is employer of first and last resort for Saudi nationals, and that unemployment among new entrants on to the job market is now 30-40 per cent, it is politically prudent for the government to maintain a large government payroll.

Finally, financial stability is difficult in a country that devoted one third of its 1995 budget to the army and security. The USA and other western countries, notably France and the UK, while preaching austerity are all anxious to sell their weapons in a shrinking world market. Responding to these pressures, the Kingdom continues to amass vast amounts of military hardware, even though, as the Gulf War demonstrated, this is of limited use. The number of aircraft already greatly exceeds the number of qualified pilots.

However, these purchases are profitable for the royal family who receive

ALAIN GRESH

Intolerance

Freedom of religion does not exist. Islam is the official religion, and all citizens must be Muslims. The government prohibits the practice of other religions... The Shia Muslim minority (500,000 of over 12 million citizens)...are the objects of officially sanctioned social and economic discrimination... Shia citizens are discriminated against in government and employment, especially in national security jobs. Several years ago the government subjected Shia to employment restrictions in the oil industry and has not relaxed them. *Source: US State Report 1995*

astoundingly high commissions. A former French diplomat in Riyadh, Jean-Michel Foulquier, claims they can be as high as 30–40 per cent on each contract. Prince Sultan, the minister of defence, writes Foulquier, 'has managed the fattest part of the budget for 30 years...he reserved the administration of arms contracts for himself... From this strategic vantage point, he watches over business [his family's] first, of course.' His son, Khaled, commander of the joint forces during the Gulf War, succeeded during his brief spell in the limelight in accumulating US$3 million for his brokering services.

The international media seldom lifts a corner of the veil of secrecy that cloaks these scandals. Any efforts to do so are swiftly stifled by western governments. As was the case, for instance, with an official British commission, created in 1989 to investigate the backhanders paid by British representatives to the Saudi royal family for the multi-billion armaments deal signed by the Thatcher government in September 1985. The UK press reckoned that handouts were up to 30 per cent of the total deal; the commission decided not to publish its report.

The state budget must also pay for the extravagant lifestyles of some 5,000 princes and princesses: palaces in Spain, villas in Cannes and Geneva, and 'an NBC [bunker for protection against nuclear, biological and chemical attack] of more than 14,000 rooms which includes a surgical unit capable of conducting open heart surgery' for the personal use of the king — to name but a few items on the budget.

Apart from this royal excess, what makes it difficult for the regime to reduce state expenditure is the social pact which, since the 1960s, has bound the king to his subjects and, say some commentators, made them complaisant about abuses: in return for their standard of living, people submit to royal control. The Islamist challenge makes it all the more unlikely that the regime will feel able to decrease entitlements and benefits and thereby risk increasing discontent.

Given a potentially explosive situation, King Fahd developed a two-pronged strategy. With western governments he has invoked the spectre of the 'Islamic menace' and presented himself as the one and only bulwark of civilisation. In September 1994, after the arrest of Sheikh al-Awdah, a communique of the Battalions of the Faithful threatened western institutions and officials of the regime. On 10 April 1995, another unknown organisation, the Islamic Movement for Change, warned western forces to leave the region by 25 June. Neither of these communiques resulted in any action by the king; on 13 November 1995, a car bomb exploded in the centre of Riyadh.

Internally, the king has strengthened political control over the clerics. In November 1992, he reorganised the council of senior *ulama*, seven members of which were expelled for refusing to condemn the dissidents' communique that September. In October 1994, he followed up with the creation of a Supreme Council for Islamic Affairs, presided over by Prince Sultan. He also decided that all funds collected for foreign Muslim groups would be administered by a committee headed by his brother Prince Salman, governor of Riyadh.

He has also instigated approaches to certain dissidents. In autumn 1993, the regime reached a compromise with the moderate Shia opposition. One such group, based in London, from where it published *Al-Jazira al-Arabiyya*, suspended its activities and returned home. But the Shia, around 10 per cent of the population, are still profoundly alienated from the regime. Even if material conditions in the Eastern Province, where they mainly live, were improved, constitutionally they would remain second-class citizens. Numerous posts, especially in the army, are closed to them; they cannot practise their worship in freedom; there is only one Shia in the consultative council. The only response to all those who refuse to fall into line is repression.

Two events in August 1995 encapsulate the crisis in which the Saudi regime is trapped. On 2 August, the king announced the most important cabinet reshuffle in 20 years. Fifteen new members joined the council of ministers. But, as London's *Economist* magazine noted, this was little more than the illusion of change. Though the reshuffle brought 'technocrats' into the decision-making process, this was confined to economic matters; all the important political posts remain in the hands of the royal family. There is little likelihood that the family's complete control of financial resources, notably the oil sector, will be questioned.

On 12 August, Prince Nayef, minister of the interior, announced the execution of Abdullah al Hudhaif, convicted of having 'attacked a police officer for political reasons'. The government holds the CDLR directly responsible. For the first time, the regime acknowledged having carried out a political execution. This decision confirmed information from Saudi Arabia on escalating repression, more frequent use of torture, increased recourse to the death penalty, banishment of opponents and so on. The government, counselled by Zaki Badr, former Egyptian minister of the interior, is treading a dangerous path. The 20 October 1995 bombing of a mosque in Quba and the November car bomb in Riyadh, are, like the latest attack on the multinational base at Dhahran that took 19 US lives, precursors of violence to come.

The final challenge to the monarchy at the end of last year was the king's illness. By 1 January 1996, 73-year-old Prince Abdullah, commander of the national guard, had become regent. Despite persistent rumours on his mental incapacity, Fahd resumed control on 22 February, allegedly because of personal and political differences between Abdullah and the 'Sudeiri seven' — the seven sons born of the same mother to the founder of the Saudi state, Abdelaziz Ibn Saud. It was undoubtedly his initiatives in the finance sector that annoyed his half-brothers and persuaded Fahd to return. Whatever rivalries may linger on within the royal family, a compromise ensuring Abdullah's succession appears to have been reached (see page 84).

But it is the advanced age of the rulers that is the most serious threat to the stability of the Kingdom in coming years. As with the Soviet Union in the 1970s, the prospect of a succession of senile old men unable to tackle fundamental problems in society or respond to the aspirations of a younger generation, can only make the task of opposition easier. The once glittering facade erected by petrodollars no longer conceals the less salubrious inner courts. ❏

Alain Gresh is chief editor at Le Monde Diplomatique, in which an earlier version of this article appeared

ROBERT SPRINGBORG

Less cash, more troubles

There is too much at stake for the government to reform the economy or cut back on public spending. But economic stagnation and a corresponding loss of influence could be the spur to political change

THE PRESENT decade has been a disastrous one for Saudi Arabia on virtually every front. It began the decade with an excess of US$100 billion of public monies in foreign investments. Direct costs of the Gulf War drained away about half that amount. Stagnating oil prices, combined with excessive military expenditures and a burgeoning population with claims on governmental entitlements, further diminished the nest egg. And while the 1990s saw Saudi Arabia replace the collapsed Soviet Union as the world's largest oil exporter, it also witnessed a 1.1 per cent annual decline in the Kingdom's per capita gross national product.

The underlying difficulty is that the rationale of the Saudi political economy is not economic growth but political stability. Material resources are allocated by the state primarily for consumption rather than production. Since there is no representation, the state can politically ill afford taxation. Not wanting to extend meaningful political participation to its citizens, the Saudi ruling family has chosen to accumulate government debt rather than to overhaul the political economy.

Fiscal imbalances that developed in the immediate wake of the Gulf War have now been reduced as a result of the standard World Bank/IMF package of economic stabilisation measures. Such reforms have been possible because they operate at the macro-economic level where their impact on individuals, and linkage to sensitive political issues, is only indirect. But structural adjustment of the economy that would result in clear 'winners' and 'losers' would have direct effects, hence significant political consequences. Moreover, for sufficient structural adjustment to occur to bring about improvements in the factors of production as well as an environment of accountability and transparency conducive to private investment, the underlying rationale of allocation would have to be supplanted by one of production. A shift of that magnitude is beyond the capacity of the Saudi political system.

Assuming, therefore, that the Saudi economy will continue to function in the future much as it has been functioning in the past, what are its prospects? In general, they are not good. The economy will remain overwhelmingly dependent upon oil, although reasonable expansion of the downstream petrochemical industries should occur. The price of oil will thus remain the principal barometer of the state of the Saudi economy. Saudi income from oil in current dollars fell from US$41.1 billion in 1993 to US$37.4 billion in 1994, the last year for which complete World Bank figures are available.

Although speculating on future oil prices is an inherently risky endeavour, those who are paid to do so are generally bearish. The factors most typically cited on the supply side are the return to world markets of Iraqi crude, the coming on stream of central Asian oil and gas and continuing technological advances in hydrocarbon recovery. On the demand side, bullish prognosticators point to the rapidly expanding Asian market and to increasing levels of world economic growth forecast for the remainder of the decade, factors which the bears believe will not override developments on the supply side. The bottom line seems to be that the real price of oil, which in the 1990s has been less than a third of what it was in the boom decade of 1974–1983, is unlikely to change dramatically in the remainder of the decade. Although Saudi output can and is being expanded, the Kingdom will be lucky if per capita income from oil sales grows more than a few per cent by the year 2000.

But pressure on the Saudi ruling elite is not just from economic stagnation. Its setbacks in the region and beyond reflect poor management of foreign policy and suggest the likelihood of increasing criticism of that management, especially from within the ruling family.

The vital US connection, for example, has deteriorated dramatically since the Gulf War and the demise of the Bush administration. Whereas President George Bush and Secretary of State James Baker made it their

The precious gift: prayer time at Rub'al Khali oilfield

business — literally and figuratively — to consult regularly with the Saudis, the Clinton administration relates to them primarily through the under-secretary of state for the Middle East, except when aircraft sales are at issue. Whereas previous US administrations were reasonably careful to consult with the Saudis about a range of Middle East issues, this one feels little compulsion to do so. Not surprisingly, Riyadh has been reluctant to fill the role Washington assigned to it as the financier behind the new US-backed development bank for the Middle East and North Africa. That reluctance has further strained relations, in part because it gave rise to a series of articles in the US press about Saudi financial difficulties and its lack of creditworthiness.

Declining Saudi influence in Lebanon also reflects the diminution of its role in Washington. In 1976, Saudi Arabia, with the tactical support of Washington, brokered the agreement that ended the first round of the Lebanese civil war. In 1982, a personal intervention by the Saudi foreign minister with his friends Ronald and Nancy Reagan is believed to have caused the president to demand of the Israelis that they restore the provision of water to Beirut. In the wake of the 1982 invasion, a US peace plan that appeared to draw heavily upon Saudi proposals was crafted. But in April 1996, as the Israelis pounded Lebanon during Operation Grapes of Wrath, the Saudis were reduced to editorialising in their many newspapers about Israeli transgressions, while the US secretary of state shuttled between Jerusalem and Damascus.

The underlying difficulty is that the rationale of the Saudi political economy is not economic growth but political stability

US and Saudi interests also appear to be operating at cross purposes on the Arabian Peninsula. The Yemeni civil war of April–June 1994 revealed the poor state of communications between the two. The Saudis threw their support and prestige behind the South, clearly believing that the US, because of its animosity toward the North and its earlier support for Saddam Hussein, would want to teach President Ali Abdullah Salih a lesson. Bandar Bin Sultan, Saudi ambassador in Washington, presumably advised his father — holder of the defence portfolio and the Yemen 'file' — accordingly. In the event, the Saudis were wrong; Bandar, Sultan, the ruling family as a whole and Saudi Arabia in general were made to look foolish as they backed the wrong, and very much the losing, horse with the US firmly astride the winner.

Washington has also eroded Saudi paramountcy in the Gulf Co-operation Council. Eager to gain support from any and all Arab states for the 'peace process', the Clinton administration has leaned heavily on the small, weak states of the Gulf to reduce Israel's isolation in the region. Oman and Qatar, presumably driven by their own national interests and desire to assert their independence vis-a-vis the Peninsula's hegemony, have responded to Washington's blandishments by receiving Israeli officials, including most recently, the prime minister.

Saudi prestige on the Peninsula, tarnished by the diplomatic obstreperousness of Qatar and Oman and by the fact that since the Gulf War US forces are no longer 'over the horizon' but are stationed in most of the GCC countries, has been further damaged by the inability of the Bahraini ruling family to terminate political unrest that first erupted there in December 1994 (see *Index* 2/1995 & page 11). Since the Bahraini government is widely seen as being encouraged by the Saudis to respond to political unrest with repression rather than with concessions, the failure of that strategy is widely interpreted in the Gulf as an indictment of the Saudis and their heavy-handed approach.

Given economic stagnation, disruption to the vital connection to Washington, erosion of regional influence and a series of embarrassments on the Arabian Peninsula itself, it is not surprising that the rulers of Saudi Arabia are becoming hypersensitive to criticism and seeking with increasing vigour to stamp it out. The truth is that Saudi Arabia simply lacks the economic, political, military or diplomatic muscle to throw its weight around as it has been trying to do since the Gulf War with disastrous results. Those in charge in Riyadh seem unwilling to recognise this truth; many others, including those brothers and cousins close at hand, do. ❏

Robert Springborg is professor of Middle East politics at Macquarie University, Sidney. He is author of the forthcoming Legislatures in Arab Democratic Transitions, *and* Mubarak's Egypt, Fragmentation of the Political Order *(1989)*

JOHN WARE

The virtuous circle

Saudi's criminal justice system is in the hands of Allah. There can, therefore, be no miscarriages

THE UK AMBASSADOR of the Royal Kingdom of Saudi Arabia looked aghast. 'In our system, the judge is held responsible for his every judgement in front of God,' said Dr Ghazi Algosaibi. 'If he condemns a free man to death he knows he is going to be in hell forever.'

In other words, to ensure a fair trial in Saudi Arabia there's no need to bother with all those tiresome universally accepted safeguards like the right to be represented by a lawyer. Divine retribution is a far more effective deterrent against miscarriages of justice. We can trust in the piety of Saudi's *sharia* court judges. According to the interior minister, the Saudi version of *sharia* is 'stern but just'.

Quite how the Saudi judges who sentenced young Neil Tubo to be put publicly to the sword were so certain of his guilt remains a mystery. Neil had been found guilty of raping and murdering two Filipino seamstresses when he was just 19. He was gay, loved both women — who were nearly twice his age — as he loved his mother, and had been alibied as being asleep with his gay lover. His letters home protesting his innocence are utterly persuasive, as was his claim that the confession, which led to his conviction, was beaten out of him with sticks and fists.

Neil Tubo appealed. But he had no idea of the result until the morning of his execution on 4 December 1992. He was dragged out of bed; told he had two hours to finalise his affairs and write farewell letters home to Manila before being driven to a square in front of a mosque in Jeddah where a huge crowd baying for blood had gathered straight from midday prayers.

In its latest report on human rights in Saudi, the US State Department says that the government 'commits or tolerates' torture, and that forced confessions are common. The Saudi authorities concede that the police do sometimes use physical force. But they say with a straight face that confessions extracted in this way are meaningless unless they are repeated in court before the judge.

This ignores the fact that Saudi courts have no power to order the release of an accused. So, in practice, the accused is released back into police custody where the beating resumes until the confession is repeated in front of the court. That is what Neil Tubo and his cellmates say happened to him.

Of the 200 people executed last year, two thirds were foreign nationals like Neil Tubo. Defendants are denied the opportunity of conducting a proper defence. They have little or no idea in advance of the prosecution's case against them because there is no pre-trial disclosure; they are not allowed lawyers in court; the hearings are often in secret; and, for foreigners, the proceedings may not even be understood because interpreters are sometimes not provided or are incompetent.

Islam governs everything in the daily lives of Saudis. This enforces a virtuous circle that allows the House of Saud to do almost exactly what it likes. Criticise the government and you criticise the House of Saud; criticise the House of Saud and you criticise Islam upon which the legitimacy of the regime is based. Those who dare to make any public criticism of the criminal justice system or any aspect of government are slapped into jail.

'In 1995, the authorities beheaded 191 persons... considerably higher than the 59 executed in 1994. There were twice as many non-Saudis executed as Saudis'

US State Report 1995

The Saudi regime also persecutes the vast army of foreign workers who have helped transform their country from a desert to a technologically modern country. Along with most rights commonly accorded to workers under international conventions, they have been deprived of one of the most basic human rights of all: the right to worship freely, openly and without fear. Non-Muslim believers are liable to be jailed and flogged if they pursue their faith.

Fred Mallo, an accountant from the Philippines, was punished in this way. On behalf of his many fellow Christians, he organised private worship in a villa in Riyadh. Here they congregated secretly to pray and sing gospels. On his way there one evening, he was arrested and he and his co-workers charged with the crime of building a church. They were jailed for one year and sentenced to 150 lashes each.

This law is enforced by the *Mutawwa'in* — the religious police — whose task is to 'prevent vice and promote public virtue'. Patrolling the streets in their large distinctive jeeps, the *Mutawwa'in* are notoriously violent and abusive. Western embassies have frequently protested to the Saudi authorities about the behaviour of what the US State Department report on human rights calls 'religious zealots' — but to no avail.

In Fred Mallo's case, the *Mutawwa'in* destroyed his piano, prayer books and all his religious literature. After being thrown into jail, he and his colleagues were flogged, causing them huge swelling and discomfort on their backs, buttocks and rear limbs. After serving a year, they were driven to the airport in disgrace, their legs shackled and heads shaved and bundled on to an airplane like common criminals.

The Saudi ambassador explained that the ban on freedom of worship — for which there is no equivalent anywhere else in the world — is justified by the fact that Saudis see their land as the holiest in the world. 'The people of Saudi Arabia,' says Dr Algosaibi 'are offended if somebody publicly practises something that tarnishes this image of...the purity of the oneness of God.'

No mercy is shown to women who break Saudi *sharia* law. They too are flogged. Arlene Herno and her husband went out for a pizza to celebrate her birthday with two women friends. At the restaurant they met a male Egyptian friend. In Saudi men and women are not allowed to socialise unless they are close relatives.

As they left the restaurant they were seized by the *Mutawwa'in* who accused them of procuring prostitutes. In court they protested to the interpreter that they were a respectable married couple. The interpreter told them they were wasting their time and would be brought back to the court again and again until they confessed. He also told them that if they confessed they would get a lighter sentence. So, despairing that there would be no end to this farce, that's exactly what they did. The 'lighter' sentence was 45 days in jail and 60 strokes for him; 75 for her.

The Saudis claim that lashings are designed more to humiliate than to cause pain and that the man who administers them holds a copy of the Quran under one arm to reduce the force of the blow. None of the many victims of lashing that I interviewed recall seeing a Quran. They all

Death of a Princess, *1980: the film the Family could not ban*

No rights for the workers

'Government decrees prohibit the establishment of labour unions and any strike activity... Collective bargaining is forbidden. Foreign workers comprise about half of the work force. Wages are set by employers and vary according to the nationality of the worker... Forced labour has been prohibited since 1962... However, employers have significant control over the movements of foreign employees, giving rise to situations that might involve forced labour — especially in remote areas where workers are unable to leave their place of work... There have been many reports of workers whose employers have refused to pay several months, or even years, of accumulated salary or other promised benefits... Many foreign nationals who have been recruited abroad have complained that after arrival in Saudi Arabia they were presented with work contracts specifying lower wages and fewer benefits than originally promised.' *Source: US State Report 1995*

testified to the excruciating pain of being repeatedly beaten hard with a thin cane that bruised and sometimes cut deep into the skin. Again, female victims like Arlene Herno were no exception.

She described how, after being checked by a doctor that she could withstand the lashing and by women guards that she was not wearing any protective clothing under her thin dress, she was called into a room full of large policemen. She was given the option of having her lashes all at once or in two sessions a few days apart. She chose the former. 'They administer the strokes on our buttocks, very strong and not fast,' she said. 'They really mean to hurt.'

Arlene told me how she shared a cell with about 100 women. Most of them were foreigners, many of them maids who had complained about rape or brutal sexual molestation from their employers but who had ended up themselves being accused of prostitution. Saudi *sharia* law contains a catch-22 vice. To sustain a conviction for rape requires not just four witnesses; all must have seen the act of penetration itself. Since this is well nigh impossible, the burden of proof shifts from the accused to the accuser. In the absence of such an absurdly high level of proof, the accuser is liable to be charged with spreading malicious slander, for which the punishment is either jail, or a flogging, or both.

Saudi application of *sharia* law is the most conservative and puritanical in the world. As a former British ambassador to the Kingdom once wrote privately, this has made the Saudis inward looking and xenophobic. The US State Department agrees. It says the severity of sentences can depend on the nationality of the accused.

In the backstreets of Cairo, I met Om Samey whose husband Mohammed is in a Saudi jail, for theft. Although she has received occasional letters from him over the last five years, she knows nothing of his real fate.

According to former cellmates — who include an Egyptian doctor — Mohammed has been given 50 lashes every two weeks for the last three years. He was sentenced to a total of 4,000 lashes. The Saudi national convicted with him was not flogged and spent only a short time in jail.

Not a word of public criticism has there been from Britain about Saudi's abuse of human rights. This silence is justified on the basis that Saudi is one of its most important trading and strategic allies and out of respect for Saudi's super-sensitivity to criticism.

Ever since the furore in 1980 over ITV's transmission of the drama documentary 'Death of a Princess' which portrayed the execution of a Saudi princess and her lover for adultery, when Riyadh has said 'jump' that's exactly what London has done. The government has taken out an injunction against newspapers preventing them reporting critical Foreign Office opinion; it has colluded with the Saudis in casting a huge veil of secrecy over arms deals, some of which are almost certainly corrupt; and, more recently, it tried hard to deport Dr Mohammed al-Mas'ari at the demand of the Saudi government because he accused King Fahd and his brothers of being corrupt and despotic.

A frequent refrain from British Saudi apologists is that because most Saudis support their government's strict application of *sharia* law, we must respect their culture. Yet some of the most vocal apologists have been MPs who have not exactly been in the vanguard of the multicultural movement here at home. And anyway, since when has popular support for brutality and injustice been justified? ❏

John Ware *is a producer for BBC* Panorama, *for whom he recently produced a film on Saudi Arabia called 'Death of a Principle'*

JUDITH VIDAL-HALL

Oil, arms and immunity

Saudi Arabia's human rights abuses are among the worst in the world. Why does it routinely escape public censure?

'THE GOVERNMENT commits or tolerates serious abuses. Aspects of the law prohibit or restrict freedoms of speech, press, assembly, and association. There is systematic discrimination against women, and strict limitations, even suppression, of the rights of workers and ethnic and religious minorities. Ministry of Interior officers allegedly abused prisoners and facilitated incommunicado detention in contradiction of Saudi law, but with the acquiescence of the government. Arbitrary arrest and prolonged detention are problems, as well as violence against women. The government does not permit the establishment of political parties and suppresses opposition views.'

The familiar signs of domestic instability are known to every US embassy official and representative in the region. Their country-by-country data in the US State Department annual *Reports on Human Rights Practices,* show no indulgence to friends. Five years after the war, Saudi Arabia fared, if anything, rather worse this year than last: the language of indictment is less equivocal, a cool but efficient compilation of offences against the most basic codes of human behaviour. Without exception, other human rights groups note a 'marked deterioration' during 1995.

Yet the West's dealings with Saudi Arabia are characterised by the same short-sighted strategic consensus that impelled the USA up blind alleys in Iran and Iraq. Neither the fall of the Shah in 1979 nor the defection of Iraq in 1991 appear to have taught the West — in particular the USA, France and Britain — the dangers of thrusting state-of-the-art weaponry on Middle Eastern 'friends' and allies. Institutionalised human rights abuses, routine repression, the refusal of any broad-based participation in government, the stifling of even the most modest voices of dissent; all ignored in the pursuit of lucrative contracts for the supplier and the illusion of security in strategic areas of the globe. Domestic tyrants in this part of the world, most notably Saudi Arabia, are spared even the nominal censure that is occasionally inflicted on, say, China, in the name of good human rights practices and the spread of democracy by western powers.

'There are no publicly active human rights groups,' says the report, adding, 'and none critical of government policies would be permitted.'

There is more: 'The government disagrees with internationally accepted definitions of human rights and views Islamic law as the only necessary guide. [It] does not permit visits by international human rights groups or independent monitors, nor has it signed major international human rights treaties and conventions. Citations of Saudi human rights abuses by international monitors or foreign governments are routinely ignored or condemned by the government as assaults on Islam.'

Which makes life difficult for human rights organisations such as Human Rights Watch/Middle East[1], Amnesty International[2] and media monitoring groups like Article 19[3], CPJ and RSF. Despite which, the latest AI report is able to elaborate the State Department document.

The routine use of torture, for instance: 'The most common methods of torture include *falaqa* (beatings on the sole of the feet), beatings, suspension by the wrists and electric shocks.' Or amputations and 'widely used' floggings: 'Dr Mohammed Kamel Khalifa, an Egyptian doctor, received 80 lashes in May...reduced on appeal from 200.' Khalifa, whose case got widespread, outraged publicity in the Egyptian media, had accused his son's Saudi headmaster of sexually abusing his son. Despite convincing evidence, the headmaster went free, the son was publicly humiliated at school and the accuser got the lashes. Not, perhaps, surprising when 'defendants are not represented by lawyers at their trials' (HRW) and 'confessions, even when obtained under torture...may be the sole evidence on which conviction is based.' (AI)

Another Egyptian worker in Saudi was given 'a sentence of 4,000 lashes, in addition to seven years' imprisonment, for burglary...'.

In rather less neutral terms than the US State Department, AI also confirms the 'alarming increase' in executions 'the vast majority by public beheading': 'At least 192 prisoners, seven of them women, were executed...the majority foreign nationals.' HRW/Middle East claims this was a 'fourfold increase' on 1994.

So what does all this painstaking effort amount to? Everything is known; no-one can plead ignorance; nothing changes. AI presents its concerns on Saudi Arabia to the UN 'for confidential consideration'; the State Department report is given to every member of the US congressional foreign affairs committee and is widely available elsewhere. This is no conventional 'communications' problem.

'Saudi Arabia is a pariah state not worth considering as a place where one can effect change,' says a UN rapporteur on human rights. 'It is the last great enemy of the human rights world.'

But there are, of course, exceptional circumstances. Alain Gresh has written of a 'silent deal' between the Kingdom and the West. 'Arabia shares its treasure and guarantees low oil prices. In exchange, it is ensured the protection of the West and its sympathetic understanding on human rights issues,' he adds, quoting Foulquier.

While wiser heads like former Assistant Secretary of State Richard Murphy under the Reagan administration, and others currently inside the US state department express concern at the long-term viability of the US security blanket given the mounting evidence of serious domestic unrest in Bahrain, for instance, former US secretary of defense James Schlesinger puts what one supposes is the 'pragmatic' reality: 'Do we really want to change things in Saudi Arabia? Positively no. Over the years, we have worked to preserve Saudi institutions in the face of more democratic trends in the region. King Fahd says categorically that democratic institutions are not appropriate to his society. Interestingly, we have no disagreement with him on this.'

As Murphy points out (page 69), by attempting to isolate both Iran and Iraq, economically and diplomatically, the USA has put its oil futures into the hands of the Saudis. Europe, on the other hand, rejecting the unilateral pressures to follow the US, has not only strengthened its options on oil, it has put itself in a better position to be bullish on the human rights front. Leaving only the little matter of arms. ❏

1 *Empty Reforms: Saudi Arabia's New Basic Laws* and *Annual Report* (HRW, New York, 1992 & 1996)
2 *Report 1996* (Amnesty International, London, June 1996)
3 *Silent Kingdom: Freedom of Expression in Saudi Arabia* (Article 19, London, 1991)

RICHARD W MURPHY

Return of Khomeini, 1979: founder of US insecurity in the Gulf

Over the horizon

**The oil must flow...and human rights and democracy are the price
to be paid for security and stability in the Gulf. But for how long?**

'DESERT STORM' has proved no exception to the rule that wars and their aftermaths contain ambiguities which need time and effort to decipher. President Bush has publicly acknowledged that he underestimated Saddam Hussein's staying power. So did we all. When the Gulf War ended, the international coalition did not have the mandate to insist that Iraq surrender unconditionally, and the Security Council was in no position to demand Saddam's removal from office. In any event the moment passed and his continuance in power, coupled with his policy of outright lies and evasiveness in dealing with the United Nations weapons inspectors, has led US policy makers to expend their energy principally on maintaining economic sanctions against Iraq.

Furthermore, the rhetoric which President Bush employed in wartime has continued to shape American attitudes towards Iraq. His equation of Saddam Hussein with Adolf Hitler in the autumn of 1990 helped rally American public opinion in favour of the war. But it also served to freeze our thinking about a post-war Iraq, with Saddam still in charge, in the sense that no-one wants to be seen trying to cut a deal with a Hitler.

American relations with Iran remain mired in mutual suspicion and resentment. Washington matches Iranian rhetoric describing America as the 'Great Satan' with its charge that Iran is the 'world's leading supporter of international terrorism'. Washington does not speak even privately, as do the Gulf leaders, of the desirability of maintaining a balance of power as the way to preserve Gulf stability. What exists today is a balance of weakness, preserved by a stated policy of promoting a dual containment of Iraq and Iran to be maintained principally by the US military presence. This has deepened Washington's involvement in Gulf security and stability. Some would argue we have trapped ourselves into that position.

My first prediction is that the existing policy whereby the United States stands ready to act as the prime foreign guarantor of Gulf security will continue unchanged for the next several years. Analyses which show that both Baghdad and Tehran are seeking, or could at will resume, development of weapons of mass destruction, convince Washington that it would be unnecessary and unwise to reassess the need for its military presence in the Gulf any time soon. This administration, and probably its successor in Washington, should be able to generate the necessary political and budgetary support in Congress to finance a sizeable American military presence there. It is one of the few foreign policy issues on which the Congress has enthusiastically supported the Clinton administration. The

USA will press for international cost sharing for this force but will not soon remove it even in the face of failure to get that support.

Two developments, both admittedly unlikely in the near future, would serve to prolong this major American commitment. The first would be armed aggression against any Gulf Co-operation Council (GCC) state by either Iraq or Iran. The second would be threats, much less actions, by Iraq or Iran to interfere with the export of Gulf oil supplies to the world market.

Even if there is no armed aggression, however, Washington has for several years opposed Iranian or Iraqi hegemony in the Gulf. Assured access to Gulf oil has also been a stated policy goal for the USA. Today, an equally important consideration is that Washington does not want to see Baghdad — which has yet to satisfy United Nation's monitors that it has disposed of the weapons of mass destruction called for in Chapter 22 — gain unrestricted oil revenues that it could devote to the rearmament it so secretly and skilfully managed to accomplish in the 1970s and 1980s.

Some observers, and I include myself in their company, find the American assumption of an Iranian threat to global oil supplies harder to understand. Throughout the eight years of the Iraq-Iran war in the 1980s, whether it was winning or losing Iran never tried to close the Strait of Hormuz. It simply could not afford to do so. In this connection, it is worth recalling the perception of the international marine insurance companies during the 1980s. They reacted calmly throughout that war to rumours that Hormuz might be closed and the world's oil trade gravely disrupted. The insurance world seems not to have shared the view that there was major risk from Iran to cargoes crossing the Strait. What other explanation is there for the fact that the industry's insurance rates for Gulf-bound shipping did not fluctuate wildly with the shifting fortunes of the Iraqi and Iranian combatants?

Military planners in Washington did not then and do not today subscribe to this logic. It is their job to take into account all conceivable contingencies. In early February Secretary of Defense Perry was quoted as stating that Iran's 'aggressive posture near the Strait of Hormuz is a threat to the free passage of oil from the Gulf to the United States and friends and allies.' Defence analysts note the possibility that Iran could try to close the Strait, even though some privately acknowledge that, were Iran to do so, it would be committing economic suicide. Furthermore, Department of Defense analysts are not immune to the highly emotional atmosphere surrounding US-Iranian relations which stems from the hostage and Iran-

Contra crises. This has produced such excesses as the public call by the speaker of the house for an appropriation of US$20 million for covert operations to overthrow the Iranian regime and the administration's frequent labelling of Iran as the 'major supporter for world terrorism'.

In the case of Iran, the Clinton administration last year decided to severely restrict American trade and investment, attempting to isolate Tehran to the same degree that the Security Council has isolated Baghdad since 1991. The problem is that few of America's friends and allies have been willing to follow its example in sanctioning Iran although they have steadily come to acknowledge the danger of letting Iran have unrestricted access to the international arms market and dual-use equipment. Some of them urge the desirability of engaging Tehran to bring about changes in its policies although few want to make this disagreement a major problem in their bilateral relations with the USA.

What else might happen which would threaten the movement of Gulf oil to market? First, political upheavals in states of the GCC conceivably could cause a cut off or a cut back in production. Second, those governments could unite behind a policy to get higher prices for their oil by withholding it from the market for a period. Either possibility can be ruled out, however improbably both may now appear.

To conclude: the Gulf states are entering a period where they will be under new pressures, social, economic and political. They want greater investment from the US and the West in general. Billions of dollars will be needed to boost their oil and gas production. If this investment is not secured, and the challenge posed to GCC leadership is domestic, stimulated by internal economic stagnation, our commitment to protect those states against external aggression could prove hollow. ❏

Richard W Murphy is senior fellow for the Middle East, Council on Foreign Relations, New York. He served as assistant secretary of state for Near Eastern and South Asian Affairs in the Reagan administration, and earlier served as US ambassador to Syria and Saudi Arabia

Excerpted from an address to The First International Conference on Human Rights and Kuwait Prisoners of War, London, March 1996

MADAWI AL-RASHEED

Mirage in the desert

One unusual consequence of the Gulf War, in a country that derives its legitimacy solely from Islam, was the emergence of a much strengthened Islamist opposition. The post-war crisis of legitimacy among the ruling group raised serious questions on their right to govern after having mismanaged the economy and overspent on an inefficient defence system. And, once the war was over, the government had to face the Islamist challenge without its economic weapons

WHO ARE Saudi's Islamists? In a country that bans political parties, free assembly, public discussions or criticism of the regime, answers are not easily come by. In general, they seem to be drawn from a non-tribal, urban middle-class background. Many Islamists who signed petitions to the monarchy in the early 1990s were men of religion, predominantly from the Central Province. Their supporters tend to be young middle-class urbanites of a similar socio-economic background: low-ranking civil servants and bureaucrats, and a group of young *ulama* and activists. The activities of more militant members of the Islamist opposition have been co-ordinated under the umbrella of *Al-Nahdha al Islamiyya*, Islamic Resurgence. Their criticism of the government centres on moral laxity and corruption among the ruling group.

The imprisonment of the leading figures of this opposition led to the flight of a number of political activists to London, the best known of whom are Mohammed al-Mas'ari and Sa'ad al-Faqih of the Committee for the Defense of Legitimate Rights. From 1994, the Committee continued to work under the leadership of these two men until its split in

March 1996. While al–Mas'ari remained in charge of CDLR, al-Faqih headed a new splinter organisation, the Islamic Reform Movement. From London, both organisations are linked to Saudi Arabia by the latest telecommunications technology. In addition to tapes and fax machines to distribute weekly communiques, the CDLR informs its supporters that contact by Sprint, MCI and AT&T telecommunication methods is safe and cannot be intercepted by the regime. The Committee is currently considering contacts with Saudi Arabia by satellite television.

The establishment of the CDLR represented a shift in the tactics of the opposition. No longer satisfied with petitions, which leave signatories vulnerable to imprisonment, torture, death or loss of employment, and unable to operate from within the country, Islamist opposition from exile became more organised and elaborated a political programme.

The letter of introduction that announced the establishment of the CDLR in London projected a dual image of its purpose and function. The first anchors the organisation in the domain of humanitarian organisations; the second in Islam. It emphasises that its understanding of 'legitimate human rights' stems from Islam rather than from other current formulations believed to be illegitimate — a reference to western formulations, though these are not spelled out.

While some statements can only be described as political — for instance, 'the members of the House of Saud are like dinosaurs. They should die out. The government is the monarchy, is the state, is the family, is the mafia' — the Committee also states that it is not a political party as propagated by the media and does not have political goals. It clarifies that its adoption of issues such as arrests, abuse of human rights and torture should not be understood as an infringement on the domain of the judiciary and courts. Such statements define for the organisation a specific sphere of action rooted in its understanding of what is permissible, possible, and recommended by Islam.

Another feature of this discourse is the Committee's promotion of the language of reform. The CDLR calls for the establishment of an independent judiciary, an economy in which wealth is equally distributed, a foreign policy more sensitive to Islamic concerns, and a strong army capable of defending the country in times of crisis. Reform is to be inspired by the laws of the *sharia* and respect for its interpreters who, in the Committee's opinion, have been reduced to the role of state apologists.

Saudi Islamists, especially those in exile, represent real challenges to the

Mohammed al-Mas'ari: a persistent and vociferous opponent

Saudi state. This is reflected in the pressures brought by the Saudi government to deport al-Mas'ari. Their strength derives from the fact that they operate on a populist level hitherto unknown in Saudi Arabia. Above all, the movement gathers up a range of frustration among newly emerging groups by providing an arena for political debate, the expression of discontent and the crystallising of opposition to the state. The mosques and the lecture halls of the universities are transformed into a space to be appropriated by activists and their supporters in the absence of other legitimate means to express opinion and discuss important political, economic and social issues. As these arenas are increasingly controlled by the state in response to the transformation of their functions by the Islamists, the opposition has pursued its work from abroad armed with the fax machine.

It is not clear whether the Islamists will succeed in their attempt to appeal to a wider audience. While the movement is strong among a subsection of Saudi society, other influential groups in the country are currently absent. Two groups in particular seem to be underrepresented: the traditional tribal groups that have been influential historically in politics, and the educated wealthy elites and professionals, who have been important in the modernisation process.

There is also the problem of regionalism. Today's Islamists are largely drawn from the Central Province; it is not clear that they will succeed in breaking through the regional barriers that divide the country. The Hijaz and Al-Hasa (Eastern Province), with its predominantly Shia population, tend to be distant from the present Islamist activists who have so far been inspired by Wahhabism. The theological roots of today's Islamists remain hostile to other interpretations of Islam, specifically to the Hijazi version and more so to Shi'ite doctrines. To many Hijazis and Shi'ites, the present Islamists remind them of the zeal of the early *Ikhwan* — Brotherhood — who, under the banner of the founder of modern Saudi Arabia, Ibn Saud, inflicted on them serious atrocities in the name of Wahhabism. It remains to be seen whether the Najdi Islamists will overcome the fears of these regions by tolerating religious diversity.

Islamist opposition is still in its infancy, best described as an amalgam of voices, all trying to render coherent opposition within the country and in exile. It is not yet comparable to Islamic political movements in Algeria or Egypt. The only common ground between the Saudi phenomenon and its counterparts in other Arab countries seems to be the well-publicised motto, '*sharia* and only *sharia*'. Saudi's Islamists share with these the ambiguity of their proposed reforms, the shallowness of their policies and, like Islamic groups and organisations across the Muslim world, are plagued with schism.

Open or violent confrontation between the state and the Islamists is unlikely. Yet there will be no velvet revolution; more likely a serious engagement of social and political forces the state has succeeded in keeping dormant for the last 60 years. One can only reiterate Olivier Roy's assessment of Islamist politics: 'Any Islamist victory will be a mirage. But the illusion it creates will not be without effects.' ❏

Madawi Al-Rasheed *is a lecturer in social anthropology at King's College, London. She is author of* Politics in an Arabian Oasis *(I B Tauris, 1991)*

This article is adapted from Madawi Al-Rasheed's 'Saudi Arabia's Islamic opposition' published in Current History, *January 1996*

ABDUL BARI ATWAN

In the realm of the censor

SAUDI ARABIA'S annual oil income of over US$40 billion buys a high standard of living for its population of around 10 million. They, in turn, can buy anything their hearts desire from supermarkets overflowing with goods freely imported from around the world. Yet, when it comes to what they read in their newspapers or see on local or international television, they have no choice. Here, it is always someone else's decision that determines what is on offer.

There are eight Arabic- and two English-language dailies in Saudi Arabia, as well as dozens of weeklies, monthlies and quarterlies. None of them is state owned, but the appointment of editors and managing committee chairmen depends on approval from the Ministry of Information; it may also dismiss them at will.

The political and religious constraints on press freedom have discouraged Saudi businessmen and financiers from investing in the Arab media. As a result, most of the major pan-Arab newspapers, magazines and television channels are owned by senior members of the royal family. Their political and financial interests are, of course, identical with those of their relatives in government: hence a press whose job is to cover up whatever is seen to harm the royal family and its allies while emphasising whatever serves its interests — which are not necessarily those of the Saudi people.

Political and religious censorship extends to the Arabic and international press that compete for a share in the comparatively large Saudi advertising market, estimated at around US$450 million annually. Breaking the rules can be very costly for a wayward newspaper or TV channel.

Chief among the political taboos is criticism of the ruling family and its 20,000 princes and princesses. Corruption, commission taking and arms deals are all equally taboo; any mention of the state's financial difficulties, or the vast fortunes amassed by some of the princes, brings instant retribution, as does criticism of the country's foreign policy or mention of the presence of US forces and bases in Saudi Arabia. The rules also apply to any criticism of the ruling families of the other Gulf states, as well as a number of allied Arab regimes.

Religious taboos are far more numerous and varied. No picture of a woman or a girl is allowed unless veiled; female singers are not allowed at all on official television. This makes for a unique experience in which, unless they are girls of under seven years, all singers are male.

A few years ago, around 30 western-educated women drove their cars publicly through the streets of Riyadh, in direct challenge to the ban on women drivers. They were arrested, thrown out of their jobs and considered 'prostitutes' by some clergymen. Needless to say, though in many eyes this was the most important story in the region at the time, it was virtually ignored by the Saudi and Saudi-controlled media.

The danger posed by Saudi censorship extends beyond the country's borders and has become the most important defining factor in the intellectual and artistic life of the Arab world. Ownership of major newspapers, magazines and television channels throughout the region has given the Saudi princes powerful leverage: conforming to their standards means stronger chances of success for Arab writers, directors and singers. Most television and cinema production companies, in their keenness to enter the lucrative Saudi market, have begun to tailor their products accordingly, at the expense, in many cases, of artistic standards. (For more details on ownership see 'The critical press in the Middle East' *Index* 2/1996.)

The scope of Saudi control over incoming material via satellite was highlighted recently by the break between the BBC Arabic television service and the satellite broadcasting company Orbit, owned by a member of the Saudi royal family. The termination of the contract after less than two years was caused by the BBC's insistence on its editorial freedom. This, among other taboo subjects, included broadcasting interviews with the Saudi dissident Dr Mohammed al-Mas'ari, head of the exiled CDLR. ❏

Abdul Bari Atwan *is editor-in-chief of the London-based independent daily* Al-Quds Al-Arabi

Silent kingdom

'The law severely limits freedom of speech and press. The authorities do not countenance criticism of Islam, the ruling family, or the government.

'The press is privately owned but publicly subsidised. A 1982 media policy statement and a 1965 national security law prohibit the dissemination of criticism of the government. The Media Policy Statement urges journalists to uphold Islam, oppose atheism, promote Arab interests, and preserve the cultural heritage of Saudi Arabia. The Ministry of Information appoints, and may remove, the editors-in-chief. It also provides guidelines to newspapers on controversial issues. The government owns the Saudi Press Agency, which expresses official government views.

'Newspapers typically publish domestic news on sensitive subjects, such as crime or terrorism, only after the authorities arrest and sentence the perpetrators. The government suppresses any news regarded as a threat to national security. However, the Saudi media coverage of the November [1995] bombing of the National Guard headquarters was complete and timely. The press reports most foreign news objectively unless it has adverse implications for Saudi Arabia.

'The authorities censor stories about the Kingdom in the foreign press. Censors may remove or blacken the offending articles, glue pages together, or prevent certain issues of foreign publications from entering the market. The government tightly restricts the entry of foreign journalists into the Kingdom.

'The government owns and operates the television and radio companies. Government censors review foreign programmes and songs, often removing any reference to politics, religions other than Islam, pork or pigs, alcohol, or sexual innuendo.

'The authorities prohibit cinemas and public musical or theatrical performances, except those that are strictly folkloric.

'Academic freedom is restricted. The authorities prohibit the study of evolution, Freud, Marx, western music, and western philosophy. Some professors believe that government and conservative religious informers monitor their classroom comments.' *Source: US State Report 1995*

MAI YAMANI

The power behind the veil

Socially and politically excluded, women are finding the means of changing their situation in the application of their wealth

THE CONVENTIONAL view of Saudi women has them discriminated against, segregated from and unequal to men in most spheres. To the outside world, their position in society appears more or less static, guarded by a fierce combination of a strict Islamic code and tribal tradition. While all this is glaringly obvious, it obscures another aspect of Saudi women's reality: economically, far from being marginalised or inferior to men, they are a power to be reckoned with.

The economic restructuring necessitated by Saudi's budget problems following the Gulf War has given rise to tensions centred around traditional values, economic realities and the shifting relationships between the genders. In their effort to keep pace with economic and social changes, and with a thorough understanding of the *sharia*, women have embarked on a subtle manipulation of the system.

Because the Saudi legal system, like the Quran itself, is open to interpretation by different Sunni schools of jurisprudence, many legal and social principles can have positive as well as negative interpretations. For instance, the concept of *iltizam* — obligation — enjoins fathers, husbands, brothers and male cousins to protect a woman and ensure her welfare. While this may be seen as a mandate to restrict her to the home, it also relieves her of financial responsibility. In addition, a Muslim woman is entitled to *nafaqa* — maintenance after divorce or separation — and *mahr* — her share of inheritance — and other forms of financial security. From the age of 16, the *sharia* makes no legal distinction between men and women in the ownership, control and use of their wealth. Saudi's extended family structure is predominantly patrilineal, patrilocal and patriarchal. Islamic in origin but influenced by traditional values of honour and shame, it affects attitudes on the participation of women in certain public arenas. But changing demographics and better education have reduced men's power to dominate women as they did in earlier generations. Women are already challenging the exclusive patriarchy justified on Islamic grounds; as they become more involved in the Islamic discourse, they can be expected to take this further.

The state perpetuates the patriarchal system; the participation of women in public affairs is not even an issue. The *Majlis al-Shura* — Consultative Council— established in 1991 as a step to involving its citizens in running the country's affairs, includes no women; there is no role for them at any level in public life, neither as ambassadors, council members, ministers nor judges. However, this 'omission' in theory opens the way for women to reach such positions should political and cultural conditions continue to evolve in the present direction.

Saudi's indigenous population is growing at four per cent a year, but the country remains heavily dependent on expatriate labour to an alarming degree. The Jeddah Chamber of Commerce reckoned that in 1995, 500,000 of the city's 600,000-strong workforce were expatriates. The declared policy of 'Saudisation' of the labour force will make reforms on women's employment inevitable. While women make up 55 per cent of university graduates, they are only five per cent of the workforce and jobs are limited to those considered 'suitable to the nature of women'. *Al-khidma al-mediniyya* — the state services — claim that women work in most professions. While medicine, teaching, administrative jobs at the airports, in all of which they deal exclusively with other women, are open to them, the law, for instance, is not.

But it is trade and commerce, particularly in the private sector, that have become the key areas of activity for women despite the segregation: branches of banks operated by and for women; shops owned, managed and patronised exclusively by women. It has been estimated that something like 40 per cent of Saudi private wealth is in female hands; in Riyadh they own 25 per cent of valuable real estate; in Jeddah 45 per cent. They sponsor foreign companies and are active in retail. Unlike other Gulf countries, Bahrain, for instance, where low wages make it imperative that women become breadwinners and where they have moved into middle

What law and custom allows

'Hospital workers report that many women are admitted for treatment of injuries that apparently result from spousal violence. Some foreign women married to Saudis have suffered physical abuse from the spouse or father-in-law...

'Embassies receive many reports that employers abuse foreign women working as domestic servants. Embassies of countries with large domestic servant populations maintain safe houses to which citizens may flee from abusive employers. In August one such safe house held 68 residents escaping work situations that included forced confinement, withholding of food, beating and other physical abuse, and rape. Often the abuse is at the hands of female Saudis... It is almost impossible for foreign women to obtain redress in the courts due to the courts' strict evidentiary rules and the women's own fears of reprisals. Few employers have been punished for such abuses.

'Women have the right to own property and are entitled to financial support from their husbands or male relatives. However, women have few political and social rights and are not treated as equal members of society. There are no active women's rights groups, nor would one be tolerated by the government. Women, including foreigners, may not legally drive motor vehicles or ride bicycles and are restricted in their use of public facilities when men are present. Women must enter city buses by separate rear entrances and sit in specially designated sections. Women risk arrest by the *Mutawwa'in* for riding in a vehicle driven by a male who is not an employee or a close male relative. Women are not admitted to a hospital for medical treatment without the consent of their male relative... Women may not undertake domestic and foreign travel alone.

'Daughters receive half the inheritance awarded to their brothers... In a *sharia* court, the testimony of one man equals that of two women.
'The government places greater restrictions on women than on men regarding marriage to non-Saudis and non-Muslims.

'Women must demonstrate legally specified grounds for divorce, but men may divorce without giving cause. If divorced or widowed, a woman normally may keep her children until they attain a specified age: seven years for boys, nine years for girls. Children over these ages are awarded to the divorced husband or the deceased husband's family. Divorced women who are foreigners are often prevented by their former husbands from visiting their children after divorce.' *Source: US State Report 1995*

management, Saudi women are, by and large, not wage earners but owners of capital, even though this must still be managed through male proxies.

This is the positive side of women's financial autonomy under Islam and a value they will hold on to, whatever else changes. Money is power and possibly the only avenue of empowerment open to women in Saudi Arabia where their economic activity is legitimised by the very best of Islamic precedents. Since the 1970s, women have used *umahat al-mu minin* — 'the mothers of the believers' — as an unimpeachable role model. Was not Khadija, the Prophet's first wife, not only a businesswoman in her own right, but the employer of the Prophet? Such precedents not only legitimise commercial activity, they make it highly respectable in official eyes.

Though women are forbidden to meet their male counterparts, own an office or personally meet men in the course of business, ingenuity takes care of most problems. They 'take tea' with other women and operate their business networks thus.

By hiding behind the corporate veil, women have been able to wield real economic power domestically and internationally as independent agents. As Saudi enters the next century, and the wealth of these women grows, it will be interesting to observe how long they will be content to wield their economic power from behind their veils. ❏

Mai Yamani is a research fellow at the Centre of Islamic and Middle Eastern Law, School of Oriental and African Studies, University of London

ROBERT AZZI/MAGNUM PHOTOS

King Faisal (d.1973): reflection on happier times

SAÏD ABURISH

Good luck and Allah bless

A looming dynastic crisis, on top of unprecedented social, political and economic problems, presents King Fahd's successor with some serious challenges

A SUCCESSION CRISIS has been averted in Saudi Arabia. According to reliable American sources, ailing King Fahd, 74, is expected to cede power to his half-brother, Crown Prince Abdullah.

King Fahd, who recently suffered a debilitating stroke, has been in ill health for some time. Although Abdullah, 73, has been his designated successor since Fahd's accession to the throne in 1982, there were fears of a scramble for the throne within the family and consequent instability at a time when Saudi Arabia is facing severe economic, social and political problems.

The question now is whether Abdullah will prove more adept than Fahd at handling the country's mounting problems. Arab and western observers have their doubts. They see Abdullah as both too traditional and too weak to cope. Furthermore, there is considerable doubt regarding his standing with the United States, the country which guarantees Saudi Arabia's security. Abdullah is known for his nationalist tendencies and he opposed the stationing of western troops in the Kingdom during Operation Desert Storm, the Gulf War.

However, Abdullah has several things going for him which may help him handle the problems racking his desert kingdom. He commands the Bedouin National Guard, the force of 50,000 which is entrusted with the security of the country. He has not been tainted with financial scandal. A simple man with simple tastes, his ways appeal to many of the country's tribes. Furthermore, he could prove acceptable, temporarily or on a long-term basis, to the country's growing Islamic fundamentalist opposition.

The real test for Abdullah is in how he deals with the Kingdom's economic crisis. Because of low oil prices and the US$65 billion the country paid for the Gulf War, Saudi Arabia has severe financial problems. It has run a budget deficit for 13 years in a row. During this period, according to World Bank figures, the per capita income has plummeted from US$14,600 to US$6,000. Unemployment among recent college graduates is more than 25 per cent. The once wealthy merchant class which depended on government contracts is suffering because government contracts have dried up. Employees of some contracting companies which depend on these for survival have gone months at a time without pay because the government is late paying the companies. There have been sit-down strikes, mosque protests and calls for reform from the country's educated class.

The economic crisis is coupled with an unprecedented social crisis. Western-educated people resent the strict Islamic laws of the monarchy. The generation gap, youth living in accordance with twentieth-century ways while parents follow traditional seventeenth-century maxims, has eroded the family and tribal structure. The division between the rich and the poor is growing wider by the day. And the country has a serious drug problem and more than 150 drug traffickers were executed in 1995.

It is impossible to exaggerate the problems facing Prince Abdullah. What he must address before it is too late are the non-violent problems undermining the stability of his country

Economic and social problems have energised political opposition to the regime. Until the late 1980s, opposition was confined to members of the Shia community, a mere 10 per cent of the population. But the crises have produced an Islamic fundamentalist opposition among the majority Sunnis. The most serious aspect of the new opposition is that it extends to the Wahhabi sub-sect from which the House of Saud descends and on which it relies for support. Favoured by the royal family for most of this century, this sect includes among its members army officers, merchants and civil servants, a substantial royalist constituency.

Under King Fahd, the convergence of economic and social problems and the consequent emergence of a broad-based political opposition have not prompted the House of Saud to change its ways. The government's response has hit people's pockets and the social and welfare services, but the family budget of somewhere between US$5 and US$7 billion has remained intact. In fact, government action has compounded the economic and social problems by imposing taxes on petrol, electricity and telephone charges while reducing the budgets of the ministries of health and education for five years in a row.

It is impossible to exaggerate the problems facing Prince Abdullah should he, as expected, replace Fahd and assume total control of the country as king or acting head of state. Also, while the country is not on the verge of collapse, the people are unhappy enough to resort to violence. On 13 November 1995, a car bomb destroyed a US military training facility in Riyadh, killing five Americans and wounding 30 others. This was the first attack on American installations in the Middle East since the Marine bombing in Beirut 12 years ago. Because there was no evidence of foreign direction behind it, this unusual happening led to the arrest and beheading of four people. However, the inability of the authorities to identify the several underground groups threatening similar action means that worse things are on the way.

What Prince Abdullah must address himself to before it is too late are the non-violent problems undermining the stability of his country. He must take immediate steps to stop the decline in the support for the royal family and to broaden it. The corruption of the royals must be controlled. Non-violent critics must be given room to express themselves without suffering for it.

Saudi Arabia is not about to become a democracy tomorrow, and the economic crisis is too deep-rooted to be solved overnight. But Prince Abdullah has a chance to set the reform ball rolling. His assumption of power without a succession crisis has solved one problem and it gives the Saudi royal family an opportunity to reform. With 25 per cent of the world's oil reserves and Middle East stability at stake, and even without family-wide reform, everybody in the West is wishing Prince Abdullah 'Allah bless' — even more so in the wake of the most recent bombing of the multinational base in Dhahran. ❏

Saïd Aburish is a Palestinian writer living in London. His most recent book is The House of Saud *(Bloomsbury, 1994)*

INDEX INDEX

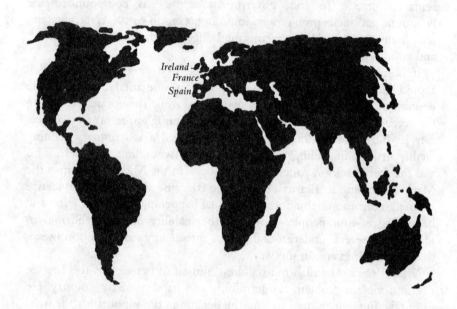

Ireland
France
Spain

Taboos and intimidation

The murder in Dublin of Veronica Guerin, crime reporter for the *Sunday Independent*, has galvanised the Irish and British press into an unwonted mood of co-operation. In an unprecedented statement shortly after the killing, the editors of a score of national papers from both countries announced their joint commitment to follow up the stories on which Guerin was working.

Guerin's murder was a cold, brutal outrage. As regular *Index* readers will know well, such things are not uncommon — this issue alone documents the murders of three reporters in Russia and Ukraine who, like Guerin, were apparently killed by the underworld powers they had worked hard to expose.

But an outrage close to home invariably looks bigger and worse than one far away. This isn't a failure of vision: the local reaction to Guerin's killing is a welcome sign of solidarity and of the determination of friends and colleagues to show that the bullies shall not win. Guerin's important work on the Dublin drug world shall not go unfinished simply because the gunmen have succeeded in silencing one courageous and tenacious individual. It's ironic that, just two days before her murder, the subject of one of Guerin's last investigations was applying to the High Court for an injunction to prevent the *Sunday Independent* from publishing her article about him — apt testimony to her determination to get at the story, no matter who tried to get in her way.

Unwittingly, Guerin's killers sent a stark reminder that, even in the democracies of western Europe, there are still subjects that are firmly off-limits and which can only be approached at the risk of crossing some very powerful interests. In Spain the issue of state involvement in a 'dirty war' against people suspected of belonging to the Basque separatist guerrillas, ETA, in the 1980s has opened a can of worms. In June the ongoing revelations resulted in the detention of Julen Elgorriaga, former provincial governor in the northern Basque region of Spain. A very senior officer of the Guardia Civil, General Enrique Rodríguez Galindo had already been indicted in May.

Now, however, the controversial Basque journalist, Pepe Rei, who works for the pro-ETA paper *Egin*, has been charged with 'collaborating with an armed organisation', a charge which carries an eight-year sentence. He is due to stand trial on 22 July. The charge has more than a hint of retaliation about it, given that Rei has been especially active in digging out the truth about the death squads and particularly in investigating General Galindo. For many years Rei has been heavily leant on, through lawsuits, intimidation and death threats, because of his work.

In France, meanwhile, the press is coming up against a different kind of intimidation, in the form of a flurry of litigation from the National Front (FN) leader Jean-Marie Le Pen. The dailies *Le Monde* and *Libération* both fell foul of the FN's image-cleansing project in June and were ordered to print rebuttals to articles which linked the FN to other far-right groups. In an attempt to drag his party — which already gleans 12 per cent of the national vote — from the xenophobic fringe to the respectable right-of-centre in time for the 1998 general elections, Le Pen is threatening to bring defamation suits against anyone who describes him or his friends as 'extreme'. ❏

Adam Newey

A censorship chronicle incorporating information from the American Association for the Advancement of Science Human Rights Action Network (AAASHRAN), Amnesty International (AI), Article 19 (A19), the BBC Monitoring Service Summary of World Broadcasts (SWB), the Committee to Protect Journalists (CPJ), the Canadian Committee to Protect Journalists (CCPJ), the Inter-American Press Association (IAPA), the International Federation of Journalists (IFJ/FIP), the International Federation of Newspaper Publishers (FIEJ), Human Rights Watch (HRW), the Media Institute of Southern Africa (MISA), International PEN (PEN), Open Media Research Institute (OMRI), Reporters Sans Frontières (RSF), the World Association of Community Broadcasters (AMARC) and other sources

AFGHANISTAN

With fierce fighting continuing between the Taliban militia and other factions throughout much of the country, local media are finding it very difficult to operate independently. The BBC's daily bulletins in Farsi and Pashto are still the most accessible news sources for most people. Radio Kabul, controlled by the Rabbani government, broadcasts only official information. The few newspapers that still publish have to contend with serious practical problems. *Hafta-Nama Kabul* (Kabul Weekly) is the only paper which has managed to retain any degree of independence. In other parts of the country papers are run by political factions. In Qandahar the Taliban run two Islamist newspapers and in Mazar-i-Sharif the papers *Beidar* (Awakening) and *Nada-i-Islam* (The Voice of Islam) are controlled by Uzbek militia leader Rashid Dostom. (RSF)

ALBANIA

Foreign observers to the 26 May parliamentary elections reported a large number of violations of electoral law, including non-government-appointed members of local election commissions being expelled from polling stations or beaten by police, and inaccurate ballot-counting with many Socialist votes being declared invalid. In some polling stations up to 50 per cent of votes were declared void. A Social Democratic Party monitor in Lushnje reported some people voting 12 to 15 times and police forcing people to vote for the ruling Democratic Party. In one Tirana district, voting took place in the living-room of the local Democratic Party leader. An opposition demonstration in Tirana's Skanderbeg Square on 28 May was declared illegal by the Interior Ministry and broken up by force. Police reportedly isolated five opposition leaders and beat them in front of journalists and election monitors before taking them to police stations were they were again beaten. Election monitor **Anthony Daniels** of the British Helsinki Human Rights Group was hit several times with a truncheon and arrested after trying to photograph the police. Journalists **Gianfranco Stara** and **Spiro Ilo** from Associated Press television were beaten in Skanderbeg Square, their camera was smashed and their film destroyed. **Eduardo del Campo** of the Spanish daily *El Mundo* was also beaten. On 4 June police sealed off Skanderbeg Square hours before an opposition protest rally was due to take place. Following international protests the election was partially re-run in 17 constituencies on 16 June. The European Parliament has called on President Berisha to annul the elections and hold a new vote. (HRW, A19, Reuter, *Guardian*)

On 28 May four men believed to be members of the ShiK secret police kidnapped *Dita Informacion* journalist **Bardhok Lala**. The interrogated him about his paper's sources of finance and severely beat him and threatened him with death. He was later dumped in a lake but saved by passers-by. (SWB, Reuter, CPJ)

ALGERIA

Two editions of the independent daily *El Watan* — on 25 April and 7 May — were seized at the printing presses, allegedly because of a report about a gun battle between Islamist militants and government troops. (RSF)

Mohamed Zetili and **Mustapha Nattour**, publisher and editor-in-chief respectively of the satirical weekly *Mesmar*, were arrested by police at their homes in Constantine on 13 May. **Mohamed Nacer Belfounes**, *Mesmar* cartoonist, was arrested

Democracy — but not yet

An open letter from a group of Albanian writers, scientists, artists, journalists and editors

'It is already clear to public opinion in Albania and around the world that the electoral farce of 26 May 1996 is the first step towards the restoration of dictatorship. The few freedoms we still enjoy — won through the struggle of the Albanian people after half a century of totalitarianism — will not be here tomorrow. Tomorrow will be too late. The old fear of the state is back and spreading. The most elementary human right, the right to free speech, is under threat. And tomorrow it may be as remote as it was during the period of obscurity we have all struggled to overcome. The free world must not remain indifferent to the restoration of dictatorship in the heart of Europe, as it did with former Yugoslavia, and which led to tragedy for millions of people.

The consequences of these events in Albania will be even harsher if the situation does not change. A dictatorial Albania could become a hotbed of tension for the entire region. A dictatorship without sufficient financial means easily gives rise to arms and drug trafficking, as well as to other forms of illegal trade, all of which have already started here. Albania could become an open wound with destructive effects on the entire region. With unlimited power, devoid of any democratic control, President Berisha could easily break the hypocritical promises he has made regarding international and regional policy, just as he is violating his promise to abide by OSCE standards. The free world must not close its eyes in the face of such overwhelming dangers. Likewise, the free world should not seek to justify Berisha's authoritarianism because it presents an alternative to the return of Communism in Albania. The last bastion of Communism in Albania is the personal power of the President himself.

A free Albania facing towards Europe can only be achieved through the democratic integration of all existing political forces in the country. What a post-Communist society badly needs is peace, understanding and dialogue between all political forces, not political apartheid. It needs mutual tolerance and respect, not revenge and discrimination. This pan-Albanian aspiration must not fall prey to the violence and lies of authoritarian state power. If this happens, it will be our common misfortune and a shameful burden on the conscience of everyone who can help Albania's young democracy free itself from the claws of the past.'

Andi Bejtja, writer and publisher; Andrea Stefani, economist and journalist; Arben Kumbaro, director and professor of arts; Ardian Klosi, writer, editor and professor; Armand Shkullaku, publisher; Artan Imami, actor; Bashkim Shehu, writer and former political prisoner; Ben Blushi, writer and journalist; Brikena Abej, translator and editor; Delina Fico, women's rights activist; Daut Gumeni, poet and former political prisoner; Fron Nazi, writer; Gjergj Pei, poet and former political prisoner; Ilirian Zhupa, poet, publisher and editor; Jorgo Balo, historian; Lorenc Vangjeli, writer and journalist; Luan Rama, journalist; Najada Hamza, painter and professor; Mirela Furxhi, lecturer; Petrit Ruka, writer; Pullemb Xhufi, historian; Vladimir Myrtezai, painter and professor; Virgjil Mui, writer and translator; Vjollca Mici, translator; Fatos Lubonja, writer and former political prisoner; Edi Rama, painter and writer; Fatos Baxhaku, historian and journalist   **9 June 1996 Tirana, Albania** on 14 May and Constantine officials ordered the publication's closure. (RSF)

Sixteen independent newspapers ceased publication for a week in June after their editors refused to accept new price increases imposed by the state-run printing presses, which have a monopoly on newspaper printing, arguing that it would put them out of business. (Reuter)

ANGOLA

Konrad Liebscher, a German priest, was arrested in Luanda on 25 May for distributing 'dissenting' leaflets and charged with 'violating demonstration laws'. He was given a one-month suspended sentence and put on probation for two years. The leaflets called for public demonstrations against Angola's appalling social and economic conditions. It was reported in late June that the government has since banned all public demonstrations. (MISA)

ARGENTINA

On 29 April police ordered **Hernán López Echagüe** to testify in connection with a request by the governor of Buenos Aires, Eduardo Duhalde, for a court investigation into López Echagüe's controversial biography of him, entitled *El Otro*. In the best-selling book, López Echagüe accuses Duhalde of corruption and having links with drug trafficking rings in the capital. The Association of Independent Journalists condemned the summons and

reports that López Echagüe was forcefully taken to police headquarters against his will. (*Buenos Aires Herald*)

Audio equipment was stolen from **FM Latinoamericana**, a community radio station based in Saavedra near Buenos Aires, on 21 May. The thieves also painted threats on the walls of the station. (AMARC)

AUSTRALIA

Following the massacre in Tasmania in April, the federal government launched an inquiry into violence in the electronic media, headed by the communications minister, Senator Richard Alston. On 19 May the Federation of Australian Commercial Television Stations announced it was bringing forward a review of the industry's code of practice, while tougher film and video censorship guidelines will be considered at a meeting of state and federal officials on 11 July. (Melbourne *Age*, *Sydney Morning Herald*, Reuter)

On 29 May the Office of Film and Literature Classification banned a collection of erotic stories which was distributed free on the front cover of *Cleo* magazine. Australian Consolidated Press Publishing was told that it could either sell the magazine and booklet in an opaque bag or remove the booklet from sale. (*Sydney Morning Herald*)

AZERBAIJAN

Police in Baku arrested **Giyas Sadykhov**, the head of former President Elchibey's

administration, and **Arif Hadjiev**, the secretary of the Musavat Party, on 18 April. During the evening of 19 April, 20 police officers occupied Elchibey's present headquarters in the Nakhichevan village of Keleki. Elchibey is believed to have gone into hiding. Addressing representatives of human rights groups in Moscow on 19 April, the chairman of the Social Democratic Party of Azerbaijan, Araz Ali-Zade, claimed that 2,500 people are currently serving prison terms in Azerbaijan for their political beliefs. (OMRI)

Around 100 people demonstrated outside the Iranian Embassy in Baku on 9 May to demand a halt to the persecution of ethnic Azeris in Iran. Hundreds of Iranians living in Azerbaijan have reportedly been arrested for demonstrating in support of Azeris who stood as candidates in the Iranian parliamentary elections. On 10 May **Eltchine Husseinbeili**, correspondent for the Azeri-language service of **Radio Liberty**, was arrested and briefly detained in Baku on 10 May, during a protest in front of the United Nations offices and the Iranian Embassy to demand an end to human rights violations in Azerbaijan. The police said that Husseinbeili did not have the right to be among people involved in an 'illegal political demonstration'. (OMRI, RSF)

Isa Yasar Tezel, a journalist with **Turkish Radio and Television** (TRT) who was arrested in Baku on 16 April, was reported on 7 June to be seriously ill in prison. He is reported to have been tortured in prison. Tezel arrived in Azerbaijan on 12 April for the official visit of then Turkish prime minister Mesut Yilmaz, and is thought to have been arrested while travelling with the former prime minister of Azerbaijan. (RSF)

BAHRAIN

On 14 April journalist **Mahdi Mohammad Mahdi Rabea** (*Index* 3/1996) was among 14 people sentenced to prison terms in connection with the continuing anti-government protests. Rabea, who works for the pro-government paper *al-Ayam* as well as the London-based magazine *al-A'alem*, was sentenced to six months' imprisonment on charges of endangering security. (Reuter, PEN)

The lawyer and writer **Ahmad al-Shamlan** was acquitted on 5 May of inciting anti-government protests (*Index* 2/1996, 3/1996). Al-Shamlan was also acquitted of charges of possessing literature containing false information and spreading it abroad. (Reuter)

A **BBC World Service Television** broadcast, showing Bahraini security forces breaking up demonstrations, was interrupted by Bahrain TV on 16 May. A second BBC broadcast the following day was also jammed. However, videotapes of the BBC film are now reported to be circulating clandestinely in Bahrain. (Bahrain Freedom Movement)

BANGLADESH

About 100 men attacked the Chittagong office of *Janakantha* on 5 June after the paper reported that the nomination of a BNP candidate had been cancelled by the High Court. In fact the case was still pending. On 6 June the High Court ruled *Janakantha*'s editor, printer, publisher and correspondent in contempt of court. (RSF)

On 11 June the imprisoned leader of the Jatiya Party, former president Hussain Mohammad Ershad, was prevented by the Supreme Court from giving an election speech on television and radio. The Court delayed an order allowing him to broadcast prior to the cut-off point for campaigning on the eve of the 12 June poll. (Reuter)

Recent publications: *Beating and Arbitrary Detention of Religious Minority Students* (AI, May 1996, 17pp); *Political Violence on All Sides* (HRW/Asia, June 1996, 24pp)

BELARUS

The arrest of **Slavamir Adamovich** was announced on 18 April for publishing a poem in the Vitebsk newspaper *Vybar* entitled 'Kill the President'. After giving the investigator examining the case an undertaking that he would not leave the country, he tried to cross the Belarusian-Polish frontier illegally, and now faces additional charges on this account. (SWB)

A 50,000-strong memorial rally commemorating the 10th anniversary of the Chernobyl disaster on 26 April was attacked by police, who arrested over 200 people. Casualties included **Cesary Golinski**, reporter from the Polish paper *Gazeta Wyborcza*. Among those arrested was **Ukrainian TV** reporter **Natalla Chanhuli**, who was released on 29 April. In the aftermath of the demonstration, censorship was stepped up: Radio 2 was forbidden by the management of the National State TV and Radio Company to broadcast live until after the VE Day public holiday. The channel was also forbidden to mention the events of 26 April or anything pertaining to them 'except in a very negative way'. (SWB)

On 7 June the business bi-weekly *Beloruskaya Delovaya Gazeta* was suspended for revealing state secrets. Since October 1992 the State Press Committee has issued five warnings to the paper about alleged violations of the Press Law. The suspension was for a report on the special forces comprising the president's elite guard. (RSF)

BOLIVIA

Journalist **Ronald Méndez Alpire** was sentenced to two years in jail for falsifying documents, breach of confidentiality, defamation, slander and libel on 25 June in connection with allegations in his book *Financial Puzzle* against the former director of the state bank, Luis del Rio Chávez. During the trial del Rio admitted the authenticity of documents adduced as evidence by Méndez, but then accused him of having stolen them. Since Méndez wrote his book, the state treasury has issued a report which contains similar allegations against del Rio. (RSF)

BOSNIA-HERCEGOVINA

The Sarajevo station **Radio Studio 99**'s bi-weekly phone-in programme *Hyde Park* was forced to abandon its scheduled debate for 4 June after telephone lines into the studio were cut off. The debate was about planned negotiations on the establishment of relations with Serbia. Two days before, lines had been blocked on several occasions during a debate on the existence of two armies in the Bosnian Federation. (Institute for War and Peace Reporting)

In a report issued in June the Organisation for Security and Co-operation in Europe (OSCE), which is overseeing election preparations in Bosnia, stated that 'inflammatory and blatantly biased reporting continues in most print and broadcast media throughout Bosnia.' The OSCE also criticised media failure to distinguish between fact, allegation, rumour and propaganda. (Reuter)

BRAZIL

On 17 April at least 20 people were shot dead by military police during a protest by the **Landless Workers' Movement** (MST). The MST, who had blocked a road in the south of the Amazon state of Pará, reported as many as 21 people dead, 40 wounded and others missing after the incident (*Index* 3/1996).

Reporter **Marisa Romeo**, cameraman **Jonias Cardoso** and soundman **Raimundo Marinho**, all with the television station **Liberal**, were detained by police while covering the protest. (*Financial Times*, AI, RSF)

Bonifacio de Andrada, a lawyer and member of Congress, has begun criminal and civil proceedings against television commentator **Arnaldo Jabor** for comments he made during a news bulletin on Rede Globo on 30 May. Jabor likened the Chamber of Deputies to a marketplace where votes were traded for favours. The proceedings against Jabor coincide with attempts by some members of Congress to speed up the passage of a new bill which would make media organisations convicted of defamation liable to a fine of up to 10 per cent of annual revenue. (CPJ)

BULGARIA

On 29 April the Telecommunications Committee (KPD) announced that all private and foreign television, radio and cable networks have to apply for new licences by 5 July. A government decree empowers the KPD to restrict licences 'for reasons connected to public interest' and remove them in 'cases of actions violating public interest'. (OMRI)

Georgi Koritarov of **Radio Free Europe/Radio Liberty** was reportedly beaten up by Kurdish demonstrators at the ruling Socialist Party May Day

rally in Sofia on 1 May. He had been trying to interview Kurds who reportedly shouted 'you have to die' and 'the police sent you'. (OMRI)

Parliament voted to sack **Bulgarian National TV** director-general **Ivan Granitski** on 7 June. Granitski was blamed for financial irregularities and poor management but the ruling Socialist Party daily *Duma* reported that the leadership disapproves of BNT's news coverage and sociological analysis. (OMRI, Reuter)

Recent publication: *Shootings, Deaths in Custody, Torture and Ill-Treatment* (AI, June 1996, 31pp)

BURMA

On 18 March National League for Democracy (NLD) organiser **Saw Hlaing** was sentenced to five years in prison after a minor traffic accident. He had been travelling to the 'comedians' trial in Mandalay (*Index* 2/1996) to prepare for a later visit by NLD leader Aung San Suu Kyi. He was denied bail, legal assistance or a defence. (*Burma Alert*)

Over 200 pro-democracy activists were arrested during the four days from 20-23 May. Many of those arrested were **National League for Democracy** (NLD) members elected during the annulled 1990 general election. The arrests were in advance of the NLD meeting at Aung San Suu Kyi's home on 26-29 May. (*International Herald Tribune*, A19)

A Burmese official in Thailand announced on 6 June that the Burmese government has tightened visa requirements for foreign journalists, requiring all visas to be approved by the Foreign Ministry. (Reuter)

BURUNDI

On 29 April journalist **Richard Niyongere** reported the killing of eight members of a family in the Bujumbura suburb of Buyenzi. After his reports were carried by **Agence France-Presse** (AFP) and the **BBC**, Niyongere was accused by the minister of defence of being an 'agent' for the BBC and of using his employment at Agence Burundaise de Presse (ABP) as a cover. An order was issued for his arrest which he managed to evade. He is currently in hiding. (RSF)

Reuter correspondent **Christian Jennings** was detained and questioned by police on 18 June and released later the same day. Jennings, the only foreign journalist based in Burundi at the moment, was questioned about his reporting but was not charged with any offence. **Michel Nziguheba**, a journalist with **L'Eclaireur** who was taken into 'preventive custody' in March remains in detention, apparently without charge. (Reuter, RSF)

Recent publication: *Armed Groups Kill Without Mercy* (AI, June 1996, 21pp)

CAMBODIA

Thun Bun Ly (*Index* 5/1995,

6/1995), the editor of the newspaper *Odom K'tek Khmer* (Khmer Ideal), and a party worker with the Khmer Nation Party (KNP), was shot dead in Phnom Penh on 18 May. Half an hour before he was shot, he had telephoned a friend expressing fears for his safety, saying he had been followed home from the house of KNP leader Sam Rainsy (*Index* 4/1995). (AI, *International Herald Tribune*)

The Interior Ministry refused a request by the Information Ministry that it close down the Khmer-language paper *Republican News* on 18 June. The paper, which advocates abolition of the monarchy, had resumed publication on 17 June after an earlier ban for insulting King Norodom Sihanouk. (Agence France-Presse)

Recent publication: *Diminishing Respect for Human Rights* (AI, May 1996, 73pp)

CAMEROON

Forty people have been held in detention since early March following demonstrations organised by the opposition Social Democratic Front (SDF). All 40 are thought to be SDF members and have yet to be charged with any offence. (AI)

On 3 May the Penal Tribunal of Douala found the managing director of the weekly *Generation*, **Vianney Ombe Ndzana**, guilty of publishing 'insulting and slanderous comments'. He was sentenced to five months in prison and a fine of US$15,000. The

Tribunal also suspended the weekly for six months. (RSF)

CANADA

On 5 May the Canadian Senate passed a bill making it illegal to discriminate against homosexuals in federal agencies and related companies. (Reuter)

Québec's separatist government has reintroduced the Commission for the Protection of the French Language after the previous government had disbanded it. The Commission, which banned English-only signs and required that bilingual signs had the French words displayed in larger letters, was unpopular with many of Québec's English speakers. (*International Herald Tribune*)

CENTRAL AFRICAN REPUBLIC

An insurrection erupted on 18 May, two days after members of the Democratic Council of Opposition Political Parties (CODEPO) staged a march to protest against restrictions on liberty and appalling social conditions. CODEPO demanded that the government call early elections. French troops were immediately deployed in the capital Bangui on the grounds that French nationals and other foreign citizens needed protection. A French military helicopter defending the national radio station killed several civilians on 22 May. After talks with French military mediators, the mutiny began petering out on 27 May. Mutineers released four civilian hostages and President Patasse promised a general amnesty for those involved. Nevertheless the prime minister, Gabriel Koyambounou, submitted his resignation on 6 June. (Reuter, SWB, *Guardian*, *The Times*)

CHAD

Accusations of fraud marred the first round of presidential elections on 2 June. Incumbent President Idriss Deby, a northern Muslim who took power in a French-backed revolt in 1990, faced 14 opponents in the country's first multi-party presidential elections. Tensions ran high in the capital later that week as voters awaited the results, with youths shouting anti-French slogans. France had provided most of the equipment for the election. President Deby won almost 48 per cent of the votes, just short of outright victory. His main opponent, Wadal Abdelkader Kamougue polled 11 per cent to earn a place in the second round initially scheduled for 23 June, but postponed to 30 June. The Chadian Human Rights League claimed in a statement broadcast on Chadian radio on 9 June that the provisional results of the 2 June poll published by the Independent National Electoral Commission (CENI) corresponded to those that had been published in an unspecified foreign capital before the election even took place. The League withdrew its backing from what it called an 'already programmed second round of elections in a masquerade against the Chadian people'. (Reuter, SWB, *Guardian*)

CHINA

In mid-April foreign reporters were banned from visiting orphanages, prisons, old people's homes, and mental hospitals in response to western criticism and the film *Return to the Dying Rooms* (*Index* 4/1995). Only mainland and sympathetic Hong Kong press with 'a positive angle' will be able to report on these institutions. (*The Times*)

Liu Gang (*Index* 6/1995), who fled to exile in the USA on 27 April, has accused Chinese authorities of persistent persecution since his release from prison in June 1995. Liu described how his relatives were regularly harassed, prohibited from visiting him, and subject to interrogation and detention. Liu himself could rarely leave home without being intimidated by police, his house was raided and his phone and mail tampered with. Two other dissidents, **Luo Xi** and **Zhang Chunri**, who escaped to Hong Kong on 21 May, say frequent detention and ill-treatment were the reasons for their flight. (SWB, Reuter)

A report in *Renmin Ribao* of an informal meeting of the Central Propaganda Department on 7 May, emphasised the importance of the 'political character' of the media as well as its 'commercial character' and reiterated a ban on 'paid news', a practice seen as disruptive to the new socialist market economy. Media leadership, said the report, 'must stress politics...and enhance political sense'. (SWB)

In spite of having gained script approval, Chen Kaige's film *Temptress Moon* was banned in China on 10 May. There have been no requests for cuts from the film, said to contain explicit sex scenes, suggesting that there is little hope of a reprieve. (*Daily Variety*)

Three leading dissidents were released in May and June, but the extent of their current freedom is unclear. **Fu Shenqi** (*Index* 1&2/1994) was granted parole in early May and is described as being 'on holiday' somewhere in China. **Bao Tong** (*Index* 6/1990, 2/1995), a writer and senior official jailed for his part in the 1989 pro-democracy movment, was released on 27 May but promptly placed under house arrest outside Beijing. Restrictions have been placed on relatives trying to visit him and reporters have been warned not to attempt to speak to him. **Ren Wanding** (*Index* 6/1994) was also released from a seven-year sentence on 9 June and, hours after returning home, sent to Dalian with a relative. Like Bao, he has been banned from speaking to foreign reporters and friends have been warned away from his tightly guarded home. A fourth prisoner, journalist **Zhang Xianliang**, was also released in early June. (*South China Morning Post*, Reuter, *The Times*, *Independent*)

Writer and campaigner **Wang Xizhe** was arrested on 31 May and given a 15-day administrative sentence, allegedly for leaving Guangzhou city without police permission. Dissidents are frequently held around the time of the 4 June anniversary, as Wang was last year. Three of the 50 or so activists detained last summer — **Chen Ziming, Wang Dan** and **Liu Nianchun** — continue to be held without charge. (*South China Morning Post*, PEN, AI)

The government is to crack down on illegal trade unions masquerading as employment agencies or workers' mutual help groups, it was announced in early June. The illegal unions, seen as anti-government, are believed to be responsible for hundreds of recent strikes demanding better pay and conditions throughout the country. (Reuter)

Television stations and cinemas imposed an embargo on US films from 4 June in protest at a dispute between the US and China over intellectual property rights. Meanwhile, the government has announced its intention to tighten censorship of foreign television programmes and to set aside prime-time slots for domestic rather than foreign products. (*Daily Variety*)

COLOMBIA

On 17 May, a written death threat was sent to the office of the **Titán Workers' Union** (STT). The message announced that union member **Jairo Alfonso Gamboa** had been 'sentenced to death' by the paramilitary group Colombia Sin Guerrilla (Colombia Without Guerrillas) for being a 'dogmatic Communist of the Maoist tendency, camouflaged as a trade unionist in the Titán

company'. In October last year a list of approximately 100 political, social and trade union activists whom the paramilitaries accused of being guerrillas was circulated. (AI)

Recent publication: *Extrajudicial Killings, Disappearances, Death Threats and Other Political Violence in the Department of Sucre* (AI, June 1996, 9pp)

COSTA RICA

On 3 May a new executive decree was published in the government paper *La Gaceta*, which declared a series of documents relating to public security to be 'state secrets'. The decree covers documents dealing with a variety of police methods to control drug trafficking and money laundering. Penalties for publishing such documents range from one month to six years in prison. (IAPA)

CROATIA

The amendments to the defamation provisions of the Penal Code (*Index* 3/1996) came into effect on 20 April. On 22 April **Ivo Pukanic**, chief editor of the weekly *Nacional*, was charged with 'publishing misleading information damaging to Croatia's image' under the new measures. The charge related to a headline blaming 'the appalling condition of Dubrovnik's airport' for the air crash in which US official Ron Brown was killed. (CPJ, RSF)

On 3 May **Viktor Ivancic**, chief editor of the satirical weekly *Feral Tribune*, and

reporter **Marinko Culic** were charged with 'rudely and falsely slandering' President Tudjman under the seditious libel amendment to the Penal Code in an article criticising plans to re-bury the remains of Croatian fascists at the Jasenovac concentration camp where thousands of Serbs were killed during World War II (see page 22). Their trial began on 14 June but was adjourned until 25 September. If convicted they could face up to three years in jail. President Tudjman's daughter Nevenko Kosutic filed a civil suit for US$635,000 against *Feral Tribune* on 23 May, claiming slander after the publication of allegations that she personally profited from her connections with the government. On 4 June the Council of Europe called on Croatia to drop prosecutions against the independent media as a condition of Council membership. (OMRI, CPJ, SWB)

Niksa Violic, a Jehovah's Witness, was charged in May with 'refusing to accept and use arms' during his national service. The charge carries a penalty of up to 10 years' imprisonment. Violic was allegedly seriously beaten by military police in Split on 16 and 17 May following his refusal to carry arms. (AI)

On 30 May leaders of the ruling HDZ announced their intention to sue the weekly *Globus* over claims published on 21 May that the HDZ has a list of political opponents they intend to denounce as public enemies. Opposition leaders Vlado Gotovac of the Liberal

HARRY WU

In the Chinese gulag

'The upcoming return of Hong Kong to Chinese rule will give the world a rare opportunity to watch Communist authoritarianism operate. Hong Kong has succeeded because of the mix of Cantonese capitalistic enthusiasm and ability with the stability of the British legal system. We have seen how the Chinese government plans to dismantle the legislative system in Hong Kong and it has begun to lay out plans on how to influence the judicial branch as well. But it is the upcoming assault on the historically free press in Hong Kong that will perfectly define the insecurity of the Communist authorities. The Chinese are determined to lay the foundation for its control over the Hong Kong people, and the means to accomplish this are to co-opt the media and put it to work for the regime. Beijing has already classified the Hong Kong media into four categories in its review of the region.

Some are already under complete control of the Communists in Beijing, for example the *Ta Kung Bao* and *Wen Hui Bao*. These two newspapers, like the official mouthpiece Xinhua News Agency, will report stories and perspectives only approved by the propaganda department of the Chinese Communist Party. They serve the state without question.

The second category are those that are seen as being neutral but can be influenced and useful.

The third category are those that have been labelled 'right wing', or mildly opposed, but have been unwilling to openly criticise Beijing. The authorities see these as needing some guidance.

The last category are those that have been deemed 'hostile enemies'. The authorities have already begun to aggressively target and attack these. For example, advertisers with business interests in mainland China have been pressured to cease all business with certain newspapers or their mainland enterprises would be impacted negatively. Blackmail has never been below the Communists.

So not only is the policy of muzzling freedom of speech and freedom of the press on display for the world in China, the world will also witness the suffocation of a once-thriving free press in Hong Kong after the Chinese take-over. We must watch this situation carefully and see it for what it really is: Chinese Communism's first casualty in its war on individual freedoms...

'China can only be changed by the Chinese. So, you may wonder what effect outside influence may have on the internal social and political order of China. Let me say that the leadership in Beijing does respond to international pressure.

I have to say that I am a little surprised at the way the world press covers China. For a very long time, Communism in China and Communism in the former Soviet Union were portrayed very differently. Russia was the 'evil empire', yet China has escaped this kind of reporting.

'China's gulag — the Laogai — has been neglected by the world media. There are so many questions that have not been asked of the Chinese authorities regarding the Laogai. How many camps are there? How many prisoners are in the camps today? How many have died in the camps? What products are made in the camps? I'm afraid I am not welcome to go to China any more and try to answer these questions, but western reporters are getting more and more access to Chinese society. Yet they don't see the Laogai as newsworthy.

To me, the core of the human rights question in China today is that there is a fundamental machine for crushing human beings physically, psychologically and spiritually. This machine is called Laogai. The Laogai camp system is an integral part of the national economy. Its importance is illustrated by such facts like: one-third of China's tea is produced in Laogai camps; 60 per cent of China's rubber vulcanising chemicals are produced at one Laogai camp in Shenyang city; the first and second chain hoist factories in the country to receive direct export authority are Laogai camps in Zhejiang province; one of the largest and earliest exporters of hand tools is a camp in Shanghai; one of the largest steel pipe works in the country is a Laogai camp in Shanghai. I could go on and on. The reach of the Laogai business was recently brought to light when it was revealed that auto components from the Beijing Laogai were being used at the Beijing Jeep joint venture involving Chrysler. I remind you that several years ago, a Chinese Laogai auto manufacturer proposed to co-operate with Volvo, but the offer was rejected by Volvo. The Laogai is involved in every agricultural and industrial sector of the Chinese economy, but the true scope has yet to be defined.

The Laogai system's fundamental policy is 'Forced labour is the means, while Thought Reform is our basic aim.' The Communist Party's economic theory holds that human beings are the most fundamental productive force. Except for those that must be exterminated physically for political considerations, 'human beings' must be utilised as productive forces with submissiveness as the condition. Submissiveness can be achieved through violence, but psychological and spiritual submissiveness are the best. The body continues to produce while the mind and spirit are retrained in the Socialist mould. The Laogai is not simply a prison system, it is a political tool for maintaining the Communist Party's totalitarian rule.

The other side of present Chinese society that I feel has been neglected by the world media are the conditions in the rural countryside all over China. Reporters have so far concentrated on trends within the major cities, but it is in the countryside that the future of China will be determined. Around 80 per cent of China's 1.2 billion people live outside urban areas. To ignore their day-to-day plight and the struggles they face and must overcome is to neglect the largest barometer of China's future. Through Chinese history, revolutions have all started among the peasants. I hope that these aspects of the Chinese story get the attention they deserve.'

Excerpted from Harry Wu's acceptance speech for the FIEJ Golden Pen of Freedom Award, Washington, DC, 20 May 1996

Party and Ivica Racan of the Social Democrats are said to be on the list. (Reuter, CPJ)

CUBA

Cecilio Monteagudo, member of the Cuban Reflection Movement, was fined and released following his trial on 10 April. Eugenio Rodríguez Chaple, president of the José Martí Democratic Block, and Alberto Perera Martínez, leader of the Peace Progress and Freedom Committee, are still facing charges and awaiting trail. (AI)

Intimidation of the country's independent journalists continues: on 23 April Olance Nogueras of the Independent Cuban Press Bureau (BPIC) was detained by agents of the political police while on his way to meet Danielle Mitterrand, president of the humanitarian organisation France Liberté. On 26 April police officers raided the BPIC office, confiscating documents. On 2 May Julio Suarez, in whose home the offices are located, was arrested and taken in for questioning. He was released after 10 hours and ordered to stop using his home as BPIC headquarters. On 24 May Lázaro Lazo, the Bureau's interim president, was arrested in Havana by state security police. He was detained for four days and warned to vacate his position at BPIC and to leave Cuba. He was detained again on 24 June and questioned about the activities of independent journalists. And on 26 June Norma Brito, BPIC spokesperson, was interrogated at Villa Marista, the security

service headquarters. (RSF, CPJ, AI, BPIC)

Habana Press director Rafael Solano (*Index* 3/1996) left Cuba and arrived in Spain on 9 May. He faced a prison term of three years if he remained in Cuba. On 31 May Joaquín Torres Alvárez of Habana Press was threatened with prison by two members of the state security police. He was initially told that he had received permission to emigrate and should prepare to leave the country. Torres, who says he had never sought to emigrate, now faces up to 14 years' imprisonment on pending charges of conspiracy, enemy propaganda and distributing false information. (CPJ, AI)

On 20 June Interior Ministry officials detained, interrogated and deported Suzanne Bilello of the Committee to Protect Journalists. All her personal papers, notebooks, private documents and film were seized and she was questioned for three hours about her activities and contacts in Havana. She was then expelled for 'fomenting rebellion'. (CPJ)

Recent publication: *Government Crackdown on Dissent* (AI, April 1996, 27pp)

DOMINICAN REPUBLIC

Juan Bolívar Díaz, director of the television station Teleantillas, was sentenced to six months in prison and fined three million pesos (US$200,000) on 19 June for defaming the head of the company Comunicaciones, Generoso Ledesma. In his

book *Electoral Trauma*, Bolívar implicated Ledesma in alleged electoral fraud committed by the Reform Party during the 1994 presidential election. His trial lasted just one-and-a-half hours. (RSF)

EGYPT

Magdi Hussein (*Index* 1/1996, 2/1996), editor-in-chief of *al-Sha'ab*, was arrested on 8 May after he refused to pay a fine for a libel conviction because he still has an appeal pending. He was sentenced under Law 93 to one year's imprisonment suspended for three years and fined E15,000 (US$4,500) after being found guilty of libelling the son of the interior minister General Hassan el-Alfi. (CPJ)

A pop song by singer Medhat Saleh was banned from broadcast by television censors in June for its 'decadent lyrics'. (*Middle East Times*)

President Mubarak decreed on 15 June that many of the severe clauses of Press Law 93 — carrying prison terms for libel and defamation convictions — would be removed, following year-long complaints by journalists. However, clauses banning defamation of the president and his family remain, in what is seen as an attempt by Mubarak to prevent media exposure of his son Alaa's dubious business activities. Despite the changes, three journalists — Magdi Hussein, Mostafa Bakri of *al-Ahrar*, and Mahmoud Bakri of *Sout Helwan* — went on trial on 12 June, charged under Law 93 with libelling former government minister Mohammed al-Mahjoub (*Index* 2/1996). (*Middle East International*)

Recent publication: *Death and Madness Threaten 4,000 Detainees in Fayyom Prison* (Egyptian Organization for Human Rights, May 1996, 20pp)

EL SALVADOR

Community radio stations continue to suffer harassment, despite a Supreme Court ruling in January against the seizure of equipment. On 30 April the office of the **Radio and Participatory Programmes Association of El Salvador** (ARPAS) was broken into and all the files about community stations were rifled. **COMPUSAL**, a private communications company hired by ARPAS for technical assistance, has also been receiving threatening telephone calls. (AMARC)

ETHIOPIA

Garoma Bekele and **Solomon Nemera**, publisher and editor-in-chief respectively of *Urji*, were detained on 20 May on charges of spreading false information in a story about new taxes imposed on peasants in Oromiya state. They were released on bail two days later. (CPJ)

On 7 June **Sintayehu Abate**, editor-in-chief of the Amharic-language newspaper *Remet*, was sentenced to a year's imprisonment by the Central High Court for publishing pornographic material on 12 October 1995.

He is currently being held in Central Prison in Addis Ababa. (CPJ)

FRANCE

In June appeals courts ordered the dailies *Le Monde* and *Libération* to publish rebuttals by organisations with close links to the National Front after the newspapers used the term 'extreme-right' to describe them. National Front leader Jean-Marie Le Pen has threatened legal action against anyone who labels him or his supporters as 'extreme', and similar lawsuits are pending against the Movement Against Racism and For Friendship Between Peoples and the Association of Moroccan Workers of France. Under French law, a newspaper must publish a response when it defames a group or individual. (Reuter)

On 3 June it was reported that the French advertising watchdog had banned a television spot which **Amnesty International** had planned to commemorate the seventh anniversary of the Tiananmen square massacre. The watchdog was quoted as saying that the 58-second film could 'bring into disrepute' a foreign government and 'contained elements that could shock the viewers' political beliefs'. (Reuter)

On 25 June a court banned **Philip Morris Europe**, a subsidiary of the US tobacco giant, from continuing its controversial advertising campaign which plays down the risks of passive smoking. The court upheld a complaint

from the French national biscuit association against the advertisement's suggestion that passive smoking was less dangerous than eating a biscuit a day. (*Financial Times*)

GAMBIA

Alieu Badara Sowe, a reporter with the independent weekly *The Point*, was released after three days' incommunicado detention on 9 May on bail of 25000 dalasis (US$250). Another independent journalist, **Bruce Asemota** of the *Daily Observer*, was released on 22 May. Neither journalist was charged with any offence, but both arrests are believed to have been linked to the reporters' refusal to divulge sources for articles about police fraud. Sowe has been receiving death threats since his release and Asemota, a Nigerian citizen, has been prohibited by the police from working as a journalist under threat of expulsion from the country. On 5 June, Asemota was arrested while attempting to flee the country and held overnight. The following day, however, he managed to escape across the border to Senegal. (CPJ)

A senior reporter for *The Point*, **Ansumano Badije**, was detained during the Armed Forces Provisional Ruling Council's (AFPRC) two-week tour of its rural projects in June. National Intelligence Agency (NIA) officers arrested him when the entourage arrived in Soma, on the grounds of his 'negative reporting'. He was released soon after, but all his documents and manuscripts were confiscated. On returning to *The Point's* Banjul office, he learned that two officers from the serious crimes unit were looking for him. He has subsequently gone into hiding. (CPJ)

GERMANY

On 10 May US neo-Nazi **Gary Lauck** went on trial in Hamburg on 38 counts of stirring up racial hatred and disseminating Nazi symbols and literature, which are illegal in Germany. Lauck's Nebraska-based publishing house was the leading source of right-wing propaganda in Germany, including videos, pamphlets, stickers and the Nazi propaganda film *The Eternal Jew*. (*Guardian*, Reuter)

It was reported on 18 May that the **Goethe Institute**, the cultural arm of the German government, had cancelled part of a three-week festival of Chinese culture scheduled to be held in Munich in June which was to include discussions on human rights with sinologists, journalists and some Chinese dissidents. The Institute had been warned by the Chinese authorities in Beijing that there would be unspecified 'consequences' if the debate with 'enemies of the state' went ahead. (*Guardian*)

GHANA

On 17 April **Iben Quarcoo** and **Tommy Thompson**, editor and publisher respectively of the *Free Press*, were again detained on suspicion of 'publishing

falsehoods with the intent of injuring the reputation of the state' (*Index* 2/1996). No charges were brought, however, and they were released on bail of 10 million cedis (US$6,700). The detention arose from the republication on 10 April of an article from the US bi-weekly *African Observer*, which alleged that President Jerry Rawlings had had an affair with Lapaix Grunitzky, daughter of the Togolese head of state. The article was accompanied by a disclaimer which read: 'We are publishing without malice, contempt or prejudice to let Ghanaians know what they are saying about their president elsewhere.' (CPJ)

GUATEMALA

Under a new regulation published on 12 April in the government paper *Diario de Centro America*, it is now illegal for Internet users to make a phone call abroad to access the Internet server of their choice. The ruling contains language that could effectively permit government censorship of Internet communications. (*Guatemala Weekly*)

On 12 May several men attempted to kidnap **Josefa Ventura** and **Sebastiana Hernández**, two members of the **National Co-ordinating Committee of Widows of Guatemala** (CONAVIGUA). On 19 May another member, **Maria Cliofas Tuyuc Velásquez**, was beaten and sexually assaulted. Members of CONAVIGUA are repeatedly accused of participating in guerrilla activities and subject to frequent attacks. (AI)

There has still been no comprehensive investigation into the murder of **TV Noticias** reporter **Juan José Yantuche** (*Index* 3/1996). According to **Oscar Mazaya**, the station's director, police waited 12 days before examining the car in which Yantuche was found. Mazaya himself is now also receiving death threats. (CPJ)

GUINEA

On 25 April a reporter for the weekly *Le Lynx*, **Barry Ibrahima Sory**, was arrested and assaulted by police while covering a student demonstration. Meanwhile, the director of *Le Lynx*, **Souleymane Diallo**, remains in detention (*Index* 3/1996). (RSF)

Thierno Sadou Diallo, a reporter for the bi-weekly *Le Citoyen* who writes under the pen name 'Bebel', was interrogated by police on 28 May and charged with insulting and defaming the head of state and spreading false news in an article in the 20 May edition of the paper, which alleged that a military officer was involved in the theft of a diamond. The paper's managing director, **Siaka Kouyate**, was also arrested on 12 June for refusing to retract the article's allegations. (RSF)

HONG KONG

Veteran journalist **Leung Tin-wai** had his left forearm cut off by two men who attacked him in his office on 15 May. Leung was preparing for the launch of a new tabloid *Surprise Weekly*.

An article naming Triad members in Macao, which had appeared in a dummy issue and was planned for use in the magazine, was withdrawn as a result of the attack. (CPJ, *Guardian*, *The Times*)

School textbooks will be revised after 1997 to reflect the official Chinese view of history (*Index* 1/1996), the Hong Kong Educational Publication Association announced on 11 June. References to the Opium War are to be purged of 'western bias', Taiwan will no longer be a 'country' and there will be a ban on the expression 'mainland China', with its implication that there is more than one China. Details of the Tiananmen Square massacre will be left to the discretion of individual editors. Fears have been expressed by the Teachers' Union resource centre, however, that schools are already dropping the use of teaching material on the massacre in anticipation of a possible ban. (*South China Morning Post*, Reuter, *The Times*, *Daily Telegraph*)

INDIA

All newspapers in Jammu and Kashmir state decided on 19 April to suspend publication for an indefinite period. Indian authorities had advised newspapers not to publish statements put out by separatist groups. Most of Kashmir's papers allocate a quarter of their copy to press releases from separatist groups, which editors say they publish under pressure. One such group, Hizbul Mujahideen, responded by issuing a threat against any newspaper which publishes government statements. Normal publication resumed on 18 June. (Reuter, CPJ)

Journalist and human rights activist **Parag Kumar Das** was shot and killed on 17 May by unidentified gunmen in Guwahati, Assam. His seven-year-old son was seriously injured in the attack. Das was editor-in-chief of *Asomiya Pratidin*, and general secretary of **Manab Adhikar Sangram Samiti** (MASS), an organisation which documents human rights abuses by the police. Das recently published an interview with the leader of the Assamese separatist group United Liberation Front of Assam (ULFA). (CPJ, OMCT/SOS-Torture)

Recent publication: *India's Secret Army in Kashmir — New Patterns of Abuse Emerge in the Conflict* (Human Rights Watch/Asia, May 1996, 50pp); *Khalsa Human Rights Report 1996* (Khalsa Human Rights, May 1996, 6pp)

INDONESIA

It was reported in May that the government has banned the book *Bayang Bayang PKI* (In the Shadows of the PKI). Published by the Institute for Studies on the Free Flow of Information (ISAI), it focuses on the 1965-1966 events leading to the assumption of power by President Soeharto. It is now a criminal offence for any person to process, publish, distribute, trade or reprint the book. (A19)

The government has put pressure on the media to report positively on government-backed efforts to oust the leader of the opposition Indonesian Democratic Party (PDI), Megawati Sukarnoputri. On 2 June army officers invited most of Indonesia's chief editors to attend media briefings where, among other things, they were told not to use the words 'unseat' or 'topple' in their reporting. A rally in Jakarta organised by members loyal to Megawati on 20 June was broken up by troops, who killed at least one of the protesters, and arrested hundreds. **Erwin Hadi,** photographer with the weekly *Sinar*, **Iqbal Wahyudin** of CNN, **Tomohiko Ohtsuka** of *Mainichi Shimbun* and **Reuters** photographer **Enny Nuraheini** were among the journalists injured by soldiers during the rally. Local stations were also banned by the government from broadcasting images of the protest or from helping foreign news agencies feed their pictures of the rally abroad. Megawati was finally ousted as PDI leader on 22 June. (Institute for Studies on the Free Flow of Information)

The Supreme Court voted on 13 June to uphold the government's ban on the independent news weekly *Tempo* (*Index* 4&5/1994, 3/1995, 1/1996). The Court ruled that the information minister has the right to revoke publishing licences since he also has the right to issue them. (Institute for Studies on the Free Flow of Information)

IRAN

Iranians returned to the polls

on 19 April in run-off elections for the remaining 125 seats in Iran's 270-seat parliament or Majlis, amid reports of arbitrary bans on candidates, summary annulment of first-round results and restrictions on political expression. After the previous round of voting on 8 March, the 12-member Council of Guardians intervened by summarily annulling the vote in eight cities, including Isfahan, where the Council accused some candidates of using anti-revolutionary slogans, making illusory promises, and buying off voters, but did not identify the accused candidates. In the other cities affected no reason was given for the cancellation of the results. In addition to Isfahan, elections were annulled in Malayer, Najafabad, Naeen, Miandoab, Meimeh, Borkhar, and Khomeini Shahre. (HRW)

On 6 May several hundred Muslim militants attacked a Tehran cinema and beat spectators in protest at the screening of a film called *Present from India*, deemed to be 'unIslamic'. The attack came amid increased activity by hardline Muslim groups protesting at what they see as western cultural influences. An attack on another cinema showing the same film was also reported, prompting the authorities to cut four minutes from the film. The daily *Kayhan* reports that Ansar-e Hezbollah took part in one of the protests to 'warn against the negligence' of authorities in issuing screening permits. (Reuter)

The Media Monitoring

Committee banned the radical weekly *Payam-e-Daneshjoue* on 20 May for repeated infringements of the press law. *Payam-e-Daneshjoue* is well known for criticising high-ranking officials and especially President Rafsanjani. (RSF, SWB)

Abdolkarim Sorush, a professor at Tehran University, has had his lectures repeatedly stopped or disrupted by militants. Sorush has a reputation as a moderate in the Shi'ite world and is accused by militants of undermining religion under the guise of scientific discourse (see page 165). (*Guardian*)

IRELAND

On 3 May the film censor Sheamus Smith banned *From Dusk Till Dawn*, written by Quentin Tarantino, on the grounds that the violence was 'irresponsible and totally gratuitous'. Distributors Buena Vista International are considering submitting the film to the Appeals Board, or resubmitting it in a cut version to the censor. (*Irish Times*)

On 26 June journalist **Veronica Guerin**, correspondent for the *Sunday Independent* who specialised in investigations into organised crime, was shot dead in her car by two men on a motorcycle as she waited at traffic lights in Dublin. She had recently obtained an exclusive interview with the leading mafia chief in Dublin for her paper. She was the target of two previous attempts on her life in October 1994 and Janaury 1995. (RSF)

ISRAEL

Palestinian journalists continue to be refused permission to enter Israel regardless of their accreditation. On 16 May soundman **Mu'aness Abu-Shilbayeh** and cameraman **Ussama Aareff**, Palestinians working for Saudi television station **MBC**, were arrested as they attempted to enter the country via Al-Ram. The two were told that they did not have the proper credentials for working in Israel. Aareff, who has an Israeli identification card, was released after a few hours but Abu-Shilbayeh was detained for two days, despite receiving accreditation from the Israeli government press office a week before. (RSF)

The new government of Binyamin Netanyahu is reported to be threatening the state-owned **Israeli Broadcasting Authority** with privatisation, in response to the station's alleged bias in favour of Netanyahu's predecessor, Shimon Peres. (*Guardian*)

Recent publication: *Torture for Security — The Systematic Torture and Ill-Treatment of Palestinians in Israel* (Al Haq, 1996, 139pp)

ITALY

On 23 May the European Court of Human Rights heard appeals from **Calogero Diana** and **Massimo Domenichini**, both jailed for terrorist activities, to prevent Rome authorities from censoring their mail and reading letters related to their legal defence. Judicial authorities in Italy had ordered the mail for both men to be censored after their convictions. (Reuter)

On 26 June it was reported that **Giovanni Mottola**, editor of *Il Tempo*, had been indicted on charges of abetting prostitution, for carrying classified advertisements for sexual services in his paper. He claims to be the first editor prosecuted for a crime 'committed daily by every other editor'. He faces a possible two-and-a-half years' imprisonment if convicted. (Associated Press)

KAZAKHSTAN

On 29 May the editors of the Kazakh edition of the Russian daily *Komsomolskaya Pravda* were charged with inciting ethnic hatred and violation of territorial integrity. The charges refer to an article published in the 23 April edition of the paper by Alexander Solzhenitsyn, in which he is alleged to have called for the reunification of the northern districts of Kazakhstan with Russia in violation of the constitution. Solzhenitsyn called the charges against the paper 'laughable'. (CPJ, OMRI, SWB)

KUWAIT

On 10 June **Fouad Abdul-Rahman al-Hashem**, a well-known columnist with *al-Watan*, and **Qabalan Ayid al-Khurainej**, a journalist with the same paper, were sentenced to a month in jail for libel, after printing allegations of fraud against a businessman. It is the first time journalists in Kuwait have been imprisoned for libel. However, the jail

term may be suspended if the two journalists pay a fine of US$330 each. *Al-Watan*'s editor-in-chief, **Jasem Mohammad al-Jasem**, was fined US$165 for allowing the articles to be published. (Reuter)

KYRGYZSTAN

Rysbek Omurzakov, a journalist with the *Res Publika* newspaper, was arrested on 12 April in Bishkek on the orders of the procurator of Naryn Region. He has been charged with 'defamation combined with an accusation of commission of a crime against the state or other grave crime'. Unofficial sources suggest that the charge is connected with the distribution of leaflets criticising the president. (AI)

Recent publication: *A Tarnished Human Rights Record* (AI, May 1996, 8pp)

LEBANON

Ali Dia, reporter for the French news agency Agence France-Presse, was arrested on 13 June on suspicion of links with Hezbollah. He was ordered to report to South Lebanon Army headquarters in Marjayoun and thence taken to Israel, where he is currently being held. Ali Dia also works for Beirut-based Future Television, owned by prime minister Rafik al-Hariri, and the Beirut daily *as-Safir*. Hezbollah condemned Dia's arrest and denied that he was connected to them, calling the Israeli allegation 'a weak pretext to justify the strangling of freedoms and shutting of mouths'. (Reuter)

LIBERIA

Journalist **Nyenati Allison**, correspondent for Associated Press and the BBC, fled the country on 3 May 1996, after receiving repeated threats. He had been targeted by both sides of the recent factional fighting in Monrovia. One day after violence erupted on 7 April, Allison fled to the safety of the UN compound, evading a group of fighters loyal to Roosevelt Johnson's United Liberation Movement (ULIMO). He was forced to leave the compound on 9 April since his presence there was putting the lives of other refugees at risk. Allison returned to work on 11 April but was subsequently picked up by soldiers loyal to Charles Taylor's National Patriotic Forces of Liberia (NPFL) on 19 April because, they said, of his reporting on the conflict. He was eventually released on 21 April and was offered assistance to leave the country during the US-led evacuations but chose to stay. He finally escaped aboard a fishing boat while NPFL officers searched his hotel for him. (CPJ)

On 29 April the transmitter of the **ELCM** community radio station operated by the Catholic Church and the editorial offices of the independent newspapers *Inquirer* and *New Democrat* all of which had been critical of the Liberian Council of State were destroyed in arson attacks. The offices of the privately owned *Ducor Radio* and *Radio Monrovia* were also thoroughly looted and ransacked. And on 2 May the **Eternal Love Winning Africa**

(ELWA) Christian missionary station in Monrovia was set ablaze and completely destroyed during a battle between NPFL and ULIMO forces. (CPJ)

MALAWI

President Muluzi announced on 14 May that he will not tolerate 'inaccurate reporting' which harms the country's image. Muluzi was responding to a newspaper report which accused a local company of giving him a free vehicle. On 17 June Muluzi accused his political opponents of using 'bad language under the guise of democracy and free speech' to slander him and the ruling United Democratic Front. He warned that under Malawi's 1930 Penal Code for Sedition people could be charged with inciting dissent against the president. (CPJ, MISA)

MALAYSIA

On 2 June a publishing firm run by former members of the banned al-Arqam Islamic sect announced that it was suspending publication of its magazines following government charges that the sect was becoming active again (*Index* 4&5/1994). At least four former members of the sect, which was banned two years ago for preaching a 'deviationist' brand of Islam, have been detained under Malaysia's Internal Security Act, which allows for almost indefinite detention without trial. (Reuter)

MALDIVES

Journalist **Mohammed**

Nasheed (*Index* 1/1995) was sentenced to two years in prison for sedition and defamation on 3 April. The charge arose from an article about the 1994 general elections published in October of that year by the Inter Press Service. (PEN)

Recent publications: *Continued Detention of Prisoner of Conscience, Mohammed Nasheed* (AI, May 1996, 5pp)

MEXICO

Six people were killed, houses were burned and several church properties firebombed in ongoing violence between villagers and local paramilitaries in Bachajón, Chiapas, on 5 May. The conflict erupted after the paramilitaries, known as the 'Chinchulines', blocked the entry to Bachajón while residents held a meeting to discuss regaining control of communal land. When community members complained to government officials they were told nothing could be done. More than 100 Public Security Troops sent to the village to keep order stood aside while the Chinchulines sacked houses and made threats against residents. (AI)

On 18 May **Jesus Nuriostegui Gaona**, a member of the opposition Democratic Revolutionary Party (PRD) and former municipal representative, was shot dead in Cuadrilla Nueva, Guerrero state. Francisco Saucedo, a member of the PRD's National Council, went into hiding after his bodyguard was murdered on 17 May. Both he

and his family have received death threats. The PRD reports 292 murders of party activists across the country between July 1988 and January 1996. In most cases, they say, those responsible acted with the acquiescence of local authorities and have remained unpunished. (AI)

On 23 June **Oswald Alonso**, a radio journalist in Morelos state, was kidnapped from his home in Cuernavaca. He was beaten and tortured by three men for 24 hours before being released near Teloloapán in Guerrero state. Alonso is well known for his investigations into corruption among police officers in Morelos. His colleagues report that on the day he was kidnapped members of the state judicial police went to the station looking for 'a journalist, in order to take him in'. They did not, however, identify Alonso by name. (AI)

MOROCCO

Moroccan comedian **Ahmed Sanoussi** — known as Bziz — (*Index* 1/1995, 2/1996) was assaulted by police in Rabat on 4 June as he was about to perform in front of striking students. He was hospitalised after being knocked unconscious. His performances, in which he parodies members of the government, are frequently censored. Sanoussi called on the government to lift the ban on his work. (A19)

NICARAGUA

On 6 June, a group of former contras took over the radio

station, **La Corporación**, run by Nicaraguan Resistance Party (PRN) president Fabio Gadea Mantilla. They were apparently trying to pressure Gadea Mantilla to register two candidates for the upcoming presidential elections. He refused, later announcing his support for a different right-wing candidate and those responsible for the occupation were apprehended by the police. On 9 June, however, Gadea Mantilla reported that the same group had threatened that they would destroy his station. (AMARC)

NIGER

On 5 May **Ibrahim Hamidou** (*Index* 2/1996), managing director of the independent weekly *Tribune du Peuple,* was taken to police headquarters, where he is reportedly still being detained. His arrest followed the publication, on 3 May, of 'incriminating' documents relating to Colonel Ibrahim Barre Mainassara. Police had earlier confiscated copies of *Tribune du Peuple* at the printing press on 3 May — World Press Freedom Day — in the first seizure of its kind since the establishment in 1990 of the country's first independent newspaper. (SWB, RSF)

NIGERIA

Defence correspondent for the independent *Vanguard* newspaper, **George Onah**, was arrested on 10 May, after writing an article about the re-shuffling of military personnel. He was released the same day but arrested again on 15 May and ordered to reveal his

sources. He is currently being held incommunicado. (CPJ)

On 28 May a reporter for the daily *Punch*, **Alphonsus Agborh**, was arrested at the newspaper's office in Port Harcourt. The arrest is thought to be linked to an article in the 26 May edition about arms exports from South Africa to Nigeria. (RSF)

Radio Democrat International Nigeria launched its first broadcast on 12 June, the anniversary of the annulled presidential elections. The station, which is to carry programmes about democracy, human rights and the environment, was created by a Nigerian exile group calling itself the National Liberation Council. (CPJ)

The police issued a public warning to journalists on 19 June against indulging in 'media speculation' about the murder of Kudirat Abiola, the wife of jailed opposition leader Moshood Abiola on 4 June. On 20 June security forces reportedly arrested several staff members of the **AM News** press group. (SWB)

Nosa Igiebor (*Index* 2/1995), the editor-in-chief of *Tell* magazine, was released from incommunicado detention on 24 June. Other political detainees — **Tunji Abayomi**, a lawyer, **Abdul Oroh** of the **Civil Liberties Organisation**, and three student leaders — were released the same day, as Nigeria met with eight Commonwealth nations in London for talks to determine whether sanctions against Lagos are tightened or

loosened. (CPJ, *Financial Times*)

PAKISTAN

Zafar Iqbal, executive editor of the Urdu-language weekly *Nawai Banker*, was shot dead by two men as he drove away from the paper's office on 27 April. (RSF)

Two photographers, **Shoaib Ahmed** of *Jang* and **Saeed Qureshi** of *Awam*, were beaten and had their cameras damaged by police as they covered a religious procession in Karachi on 27 May. (Pakistan Press Foundation)

PALESTINE (AUTONOMOUS AREAS)

Iyad Sarraj, a psychiatrist and head of the **Palestinian Independent Commission for Citizens' Rights** (PICCR), was arrested at his home in Gaza by plainclothes police on 9 June, after sending a letter to President Arafat criticising a security crackdown by the Palestinian National Authority in which around 900 people were arrested. The next day police raided and closed his office at the Gaza Community Mental Health Programme, confiscating files and videotapes. On 13 June Sarraj was charged with assaulting a police officer while in custody and with drug dealing, after hashish was allegedly found at his office. In a letter smuggled out of jail Sarraj claimed that he had been beaten while in detention, a claim backed up by his bruised appearance in court, and the fact that the police officer he is alleged to have assaulted had a bandaged fist. A civil court dropped the drugs charges but a military court ordered him to be remanded in jail for assault. He was released on 26 June, shortly before he was due to answer the assault charge in court. (*Middle East International*, Reuter)

PERU

Police broke up a strike by municipal employees in Lima on 3 May. Journalists from the magazine *Caretas,* the daily *El Comercio* and several television stations who were covering the protest were injured in the attack. A judicial inquiry has been ordered into the police handling of the strike. (IPYS)

On 22 May **Adolfo Fasanando**, Panamericana Television's correspondent in Tarapoto, was questioned by police in connection with an interview he conducted with an alleged drug trafficker. He was pressed to reveal the identity of the interviewee, but refused. Since being questioned, Fasanando reports being constantly followed near his home and the television network's offices. (IPYS)

Radio Oriental reporter **Miguel Pérez Julca**, who was arrested on terrorism charges in 1992, was released from prison on 8 June after the intervention of congress-woman and journalist Elferez Vidarte. Vidarte contacted the Congressional Human Rights and Pacification Commission and state prosecutor Blanca Nelida Colan in order to secure his release. (IPYS)

Julio Alberto Quevedo

Chávez of the magazine *El Tarapotino*, **Luis Humberto Hidalgo Sánchez** of **Radio Tarapoto** and **Cesar Herrera Luna** of the magazine *El Achichito* were charged in June with defaming the former manager of the water treatment service in the city of Tarapoto, Carlo Magno Pasquel Cárdenas. All three journalists had criticised a 50 per cent increase in water rates in the city, alluding to Pasqual's supposed links to terrorist organisations. The journalists are currently on 'conditional freedom', unable to leave Tarapoto without permission or to stay outside later than 10pm. (IPYS)

QATAR

The daily *As Sharq* was suspended for three months by the Ministry of Information and Culture on 26 June, for publishing a poem by an Islamist from Saudi Arabia in its 17 June edition. The poem 'undermined the heads of state and damaged relations with other friendly Arab countries', according to the Ministry. (RSF)

ROMANIA

On 7 May Adrian Nastase, president of the Chamber of Deputies and executive president of the ruling Party of Social Democracy, asked the National Audio-Visual Council (CNA) to reconsider the frequency allocation of those radio stations which rebroadcast material from the **BBC**. He alleged that the BBC's coverage of Romania's elections was biased in favour of opposition parties. The

same day **Liviu Man**, the BBC's Cluj correspondent, received anonymous threatening telephone calls telling him to cease reporting 'incidents that incriminated President Iliescu'. The calls may relate to Man's report about assaults on protesters during Iliescu's visit to Cluj on 3 May. (CPJ, IFJ, RSF)

At a press conference on 13 May **Captain Constantin Bucur** of the Romanian Intelligence Service (SRI) played tapes of conversations between politicians and other public figures which, he alleged, were obtained by the SRI with illegal telephone taps. Bucur is to be prosecuted for revealing intelligence secrets, and could face seven years in jail if convicted. On 14 May Parliament approved a law restricting telephone tapping by the security services to cases where a warrant has been obtained. (Reuter, OMRI)

RUSSIAN FEDERATION

Russia: A Moscow court ruled in favour of the Culture Ministry on 6 May in a lawsuit brought against *Pravda* newspaper and journalist **Vladimir Teteryatnikov**. Teteryatnikov had published a number of articles alleging that the Ministry's stand on the future of cultural treasures brought to Russia from Germany after World War II was anti-Russian and pro-German, and in particular alleging 'the incompetence of officialdom acting in the name of culture'. *Pravda* was ordered to publish a denial and pay compensation. (SWB)

At a meeting with leaders of regional media on 6 May President Yeltsin said freedom of speech is now a 'reality' in Russia and that protection for the press against 'criminal commercial organisations' is a top priority. (SWB)

The crime reporter for the Siberian daily *Zabaikalsky Rabochy*, Viktor Mikhailov, was killed and mutilated by unknown assailants in broad daylight in Chita on 12 May. He had been covering the work of law enforcement agencies at the time of his murder. Thirteen journalists have now been killed in Federation territory since 1994. The murder of *Obshchaya Gazeta* journalist Nadezhda Chaikova (*Index* 3/1996) has still not been formally investigated by the prosecutor-general. (CPJ)

A crew from NTV was prevented from filming the departure of a State Duma delegation to North Korea on 26 May. In Pyongyang, meanwhile, the North Korean authorities announced that the correspondents of leading Russian news agencies who were to cover the visit had been denied visas to enter the country. The Russian Foreign Ministry said that it 'does not intend to ignore the refusal of visas'. (SWB)

Chechnya: On 8 May Nina Yefimova, a reporter for the Russian-language paper *Vozrozhdeniye* (Revival), was abducted from her apartment in Grozny, together with her mother. She was found dead the following morning from a pistol shot to the back of the head. Her mother was found that evening in a deserted canned food factory in Grozny. Journalists in Grozny and Moscow believe that the murders are connected to stories Yefimova had published on crime in Chechnya. (CPJ)

A TV crew from Associated Press was attacked by armed men in the vicinity of Grozny on 17 June. They were robbed of money and valuables and told: 'All journalists are spies and you will have to be killed.' The crew made their escape, however, when their attackers' car failed to start. (SWB)

North Ossetia: North Ossetian post offices stopped delivering the free anti-Communist newspaper *Nie Dai Bog* (God Forbid) on 27 May after the local electoral office advised that delivering it broke the law forbidding government organisations from taking part in election campaigns. (SWB)

Tatarstan: A decree issued on 24 June forbids making insulting or slanderous public remarks about the president and provides for a minimum fine of four million rubles (US$800) for anyone who does so. Any publication reporting such an insult will be fined 30 million rubles and have all copies of the offending issue confiscated. (CPJ)

Recent publications: *Open Letter from Amnesty International to the Presidential Candidates on the Occasion of the Presidential Elections* (AI, June 1996, 9pp); *Briefing on Press Freedom in Russia Before the Presidential Elections* (CPJ, June 1996, 16pp)

RWANDA

The first three defendants appeared before the international war crimes tribunal in Tanzania on 31 May and 2 June. They are Clement Kayishema, former governor of Kibuye province (which had the highest concentration of Tutsis in Rwanda before the genocide), George Anderson Rutaganda, former vice-president of the Interahamwe militias, and Jean Paul Akayesu, a former mayor in Giterama province. The first trial is scheduled to start on September 26. Meanwhile, exiled Hutu politicians have stepped up their campaign to force the government in Kigali to pass a mass amnesty for those accused of genocide. (Reuter, SWB, *Guardian*)

The Rwandan Information Office (ORINFOR) admitted in early May that disappeared journalist Joseph Runyezi (*Index* 3/1996) is being held at Kigali Central Prison on suspicion of committing rape and mutilation during the genocide. Other sources, however, cast serious doubt on the validity of the allegations and there are fears that he may be tortured while in detention. (AI)

SERBIA-MONTENEGRO

Serbia: The Municipality of Smederevo announced a take-over of the independent station Radio Smederevo on 30 May, by increasing its share of ownership from 17 per cent to 63 per cent. The station's premises were occupied and the electricity cut off. A new board and management were installed, all members of the ruling Socialist Party. Radio Smederevo was the only independent electronic medium in the region. (CPJ)

On 7 June the financial inspector for the city of Pancevo, reportedly acting on the instructions of the ruling Socialist Party, told *Novi Pancevac* journalists that their work permits were no longer valid, thereby effectively preventing them from operating. (RSF)

Kosovo: On 2 April **Enver Grajcevci** was arrested with a bag containing 200 copies of a magazine called *Clirimi* (Liberation), apparently issued by the National Movement for the Liberation of Kosovo, which advocates Kosovo's reunification with Albania by force of arms. Grajcevci was reportedly tortured by electric shocks while in detention and may face charges of 'calling for the violent change of the constitutional order'. (OMRI)

On 11 April police reportedly detained **Ahmet Kurtolli**, marketing director of the weekly *Koha*. Kurtolli was questioned about the latest issue of the paper, which was originally banned (*Index* 3/1996) but appeared in kiosks a week later. After international protests the prosecutor-general revoked an earlier order stating that the paper cannot be published without prior vetting. (OMRI)

Recent publication: *Spotlight On Human Rights in Serbia and Montenegro* (Humanitarian Law Center, 1996, 164pp)

SLOVENIA

On 30 May **Bernard Nezmah** of the weekly *Mladina* was given a one-month suspended sentence and fined under Article 169 of the Civil Code, which relates to 'insulting' comments made by the press. The suit was brought by former foreign affairs minister Dimitri Rupel who was criticised, along with the mayor of Ljubljuana, in a February 1995 article. (RSF)

SOLOMON ISLANDS

The board of directors of the Solomon Islands Broadcasting Corporation (SIBC) announced on 14 May that all news items and current affairs programmes must be screened by the general manager, James Kilua, before broadcast. The policy change arose from a news report about the discovery of a bomb at Honiara's Henderson Airport. The government denied the report and reportedly pressured the SIBC board to control the activities of news staff. (SWB)

SOUTH KOREA

In mid-June former union leader **Choi Moon-sung** and several other former union officials at the Munhwa Broadcasting Corporation were suspended from office for six months for taking part in a strike protesting against the reappointment of Kang Sung-koo as the network's president in March (*Index* 3/1996). Following mass resignations at the network, Kang Sung-koo himself resigned on 15 June. (Reuter)

Kim Dong-won of the independent **Purn Production** television company was arrested on 14 June and charged under the Audio and Video Censorship Act with failing to submit to prior censorship procedures. (AMARC)

SPAIN

Pepe Rei (*Index* 5/1995), an investigative journalist with the Basque separatist paper *Egin*, has been charged with 'collaborating with an armed organisation'. Rei has been at the forefront of investigations into state-sponsored death squad activity against suspected members and symnpathisers of the separatist guerrilla group ETA during the 1980s. He is due to stand trial on 22 July and faces a possible eight-year sentence if convicted. (*Nuevo Amanecer*)

Recent publication: *Comments by Amnesty International on the Government's Fourth Periodic Report to the Human Rights Committee* (AI, April 1996, 15pp)

SRI LANKA

The Department of Information on 11 May lifted the ban on news broadcasts by Sirasa FM (*Index* 3/1996). Two journalists — news director **Sugeeswara Senadheera** and news editor **Ranjith Amerasinghe** — were charged with bringing the government into disrepute and broadcasting false news. They were also threatened with charges for causing panic and disaffection. The MBC network, which runs Sirasa

FM, dismissed the journalists and denied all responsibility for their actions, and has refused to provide them with legal assistance. (Reuter, Free Media Movement)

The Sunday Leader of 12 May published a report alleging that Edmond Jayasinghe, secretary to the Media Ministry and government censor of publications, had fraudulently obtained appointments in the public service by falsifying his date of birth on official documents. His year of birth is recorded variously as 1940, 1944 and 1946. The Free Media Movement (FMM) called for Jayasinghe's immediate resignation. (FMM)

SUDAN

Sudanese security forces arrested four journalists with state-owned **Sudanese Television** in late April. News director **Ismael Muhammad al-Hussein**, news editors **Hussein Saleh** and **Abbas Suleiman**, and cameraman **Osama Ghandi** were arrested at the station's offices. There has been no news of the journalists since their arrests and it is feared that they are being held in 'ghost houses' where torture is routine. (CPJ)

On 20 May a group of armed men stormed the offices of the independent daily *al-Rai al-Akhar* and confiscated all 20,000 copies of that day's edition. The raid occurred a day after the paper reported a revolt at a prison south of Khartoum, a report denied by the authorities. The paper was subsequently suspended for two weeks. (RSF, Reuter)

Recent publication: *Progress or Public Relations?* (AI, May 1996, 37pp)

SWAZILAND

On a visit to state-run radio and television newsrooms on 23 June, acting prime minister Sishayi Nxumalo demanded the removal of reports on a clash between police and striking teachers. At one point, Nxumalo interrupted the live news bulletin on **Radio Swaziland** and ordered the newscaster to stop reading. On 24 June the privately owned *Times of Swaziland* received a letter from Nxumalo threatening legal action after it reported his intervention of the previous day. (MISA)

TAJIKSTAN

Two unnamed Tajik Democratic Party (DPT) representatives were reported to have been arrested on 1 May, apparently for 'spreading anti-government propaganda' and possessing copies of the newspaper *Charogi Ruz*. They were released about a week later. (SWB)

Reporters in the northern Leninabad region were prevented from filming or transmitting video despatches about unrest between local residents and government officials on 15 May. (SWB)

Recent publication: *Tajik Refugees in Northern Afghanistan — Obstacles to Repatriation* (HRW, May 1996, 35pp)

TIBET

The official Chinese-language *Tibet Daily* announced a ban on photos and likenesses (including pictures on watches and pens) of the Dalai Lama in religious institutions in April. This was later extended to secular establishments and plainclothes policemen visited hotels, restaurants, and shops in search of the photos — now classified as 'reactionary propaganda' — on 22 and 23 April. On 16 May secondary-school children in Lhasa were told that possessing photos of the religious leader was no longer permitted and the wearing of *sung du* (red cords commonly worn by Tibetan Buddhists) was also banned. Four days later, house-to-house searches for photos were carried out and government employees in Lhasa were required to sign a statement listing the number of photos of the Dalai Lama in their possession. (Tibet Information Network)

Ganden monastery was closed and around 90 of its members detained in Gusta prison after fighting broke out between monks and members of an official Work Team sent to announce the ban on photos of the Dalai Lama on 6 May. Many monks were injured in raids carried out on 7 and 10 May and one, **Kelsang Nyendrak**, died of gunshot wounds. Two of Lhasa's main monasteries, Drepung and Jokhang, closed on 12 and 14 May respectively in protest at the ban and monks were reportedly beaten at Sera and Ramoche during protests on 13 and 14 May. Meanwhile, a Japanese tourist reported seeing some 80 wounded people, mainly monks and nuns, arrive at Lhasa People's Hospital, the result of a police crackdown against Tibetan unrest. (Tibet Information Network)

On 27 May five Tibetans — named as **Tsering Lhamo, Ngawang Kelsang, Buchung, Damchoe and Nyima Dondrup** — were imprisoned for up to five years in the first officially acknowledged political trial for two years for calling for Tibetan independence. (Tibet Information Network)

China admitted for the first time on 28 May that it has been holding the missing Tibetan child **Gendun Choekyi Nyima**, the Dalai Lama's disputed choice of **Panchen Lama** (*Index* 5/1995). China's UN ambassador said that the child was put under government protection at the request of his parents and to protect him from being kidnapped by Tibetan nationalists. (Tibet Information Network)

On 14 June **Ken Ali**, editor of the *Mirror*, was jailed for 14 days and **Sharmain Baboolah** of the same paper was fined US$1,000 for contempt of court. The *Mirror* was judged to have broken a series of injunctions placing restrictions on press coverage of a murder trial in Chaguaramas. The trial judge also ordered the press not to report on the sentence against Ali. He was released on bail after five days in prison and has appealed against his sentence. The *Mirror* and the *Independent* have brought a

constitutional motion alleging that the trial judge's restrictions violated the right to freedom of expression as guaranteed in the constitution. (Trinidad *Independent*)

TUNISIA

Mohamed Mouadda, leader of opposition **Movement of Democratic Socialists** (MDS), was sentenced to 11 years' imprisonment on 29 February, on a charge of 'associating with agents of a foreign power aiming to undermine Tunisia'. An AI observer said that the trial was unfair and Mouadda's defence was prevented from calling witnesses. **Frej Frenniche**, executive director of the Arab Institute of Human Rights, was detained for four days after being arrested at Tunis airport on 10 May en route to France. He is reportedly being investigated on charges of carrying documents deemed to be defamatory and insulting to the authorities. His passport was also seized. On 18 May **Khemais Chammari**, a human rights activist and MDS member of Parliament, was arrested. It is believed that his arrest is connected to the documents found on Frej Frenniche which were written by Chammari, condemning the human rights situation in Tunisia and intended for a human rights meeting in France. And **Patrick Baudoin**, head of the International Federation of Human Rights, was forced to fly back to Paris after being labelled an 'undesirable' by the Tunisian authorities when he landed in Tunis on 23 May. (AI, *Guardian*)

The Tunisian embassy in Paris refused in May to renew the passport of **Salah Bechir**, journalist with the London-based Arabic-language daily *al-Hayat*. **Kamel Labidi**, Tunis correspondent for French daily *La Croix-L'Evenement*, is still waiting for the return of his passport, confiscated in January. (RSF)

TURKEY

On 18 April Istanbul State Security Court ordered the left-wing daily *Evrensel* (Universal) closed for 10 days for publishing the statement of a terrorist organisation, in violation of Article 7 of the Anti-Terror Law (*Index* 2/1996, 3/1996). The charge stems from an article published in the paper on 29 October 1995 about the Revolutionary Front of the People's Liberation Party (DHKPC). On 9 May the court ordered a further 20-day closure in connection with an article entitled 'Confessions of a Military Officer', which allegedly incited racism. (CPJ)

On 3 May four journalists — **Sabiha Budak, Incigül Basel, Mehtap Kurucay** and **Filiz Öztürk** — from the leftist weekly *Alinteri* (Toil) were beaten and arrested by Istanbul police. Basel was released the following day; the other three were released on 19 May. Kurucay is reported to have been tortured in detention. (RSF, AI)

On 15 May writer and journalist **Haluk Gerger** was sentenced by an Istanbul court to 20 months in prison and fined TL 500,000 (US$6) for an article published in the 30 June 1995 edition of *Evrensel* on the state of emergency in southeast Turkey (*Index* 1/1995, 5/1995, 6/1995, 1/1996). In the same trial **Fatma Bayer**, *Evrensel*'s former editor-in-chief, was also sentenced to 20 months in prison (*Index* 2/1996, 3/1996). The sentence was later commuted to a fine of TL 3.5 million. Both were sentenced under Article 312 of the Penal Code for 'inciting racism'. (PEN)

On 21 May a court ordered the left-wing weekly *Aydinlik* (Light) to remove an interview it intended to print with a leader of Turkey's criminal underworld. The article contained allegations that Mehmet Agar, the current minister of justice and former national police chief, has ties with organised crime. Although *Aydinlik* complied with the court order, the issue was seized at the printers on 24 May after a judge had ruled that the paper was 'pornographic'. The following week's issue was also seized. This time a judge ruled that an article about the previous confiscation, entitled 'Are the Judges Mehmet Agar's Personal Bodyguards?', insulted the judiciary. (CPJ)

At the beginning of June the Islamist-run town council of Kayseri in central Turkey banned *Istanbul Beneath My Wings*, a popular Turkish film which portrays a seventeenth-century sultan as bisexual. The mayor of Kayseri, Sükrü Karatepe, said the film 'approaches our history from a distorted viewpoint'. The film

traces Hazerfen Ahmet Celebi's experimentation and eventual flight across the Bosphorus with makeshift wings during the reign of Sultan Murat IV. (Reuter)

Recent publication: *Trade Unionists Face Persecution* (AI, April 1996, 4pp)

UKRAINE

On 10 May the body of journalist **Igor Grouchetsky** was found on a street near his home in the ciy of Tcherkassy, southwest of Kiev. He was the Tcherkassy correspondent for the Kiev newspaper *Ukraine-Centre* and well known for his reports on crime and corruption in the country. Shortly before his death, he had testified in a criminal case involving, among others, the son of a high-ranking police official in Tcherkassy. (RSF)

Six anonymous articles were published in pro-government papers in June, attacking leading independent journalists. An article in *Nezavissimost* on 11 June attacked *Business* journalist **Dmitri Djanguirov** for his Armenian origins in order to discredit his criticism of presidential policy. The same day an article appeared in *Pravda Ukraina* attacking *Silski Visti* deputy editor **Ivan Boki**. Two days later the paper published an article attacking the deputy editor of the weekly *Zerkalo Nedeli*, **Julia Mostavaia**. The article said Mostvaia 'buys her clothes in Tel Aviv' and described her paper as a 'fifth column' because it is sold in the US. (RSF)

UNITED ARAB EMIRATES

A rare public row broke out in June between the telecommunications company Etisalat (of which the government owns 60 per cent) and the Dubai police chief, Major-General Dhahi Khalfan Tamim, over regulating access to the Internet. Etisalat general manager Ali Salim al-Owais said the firm had pulled its representative from the government body overseeing the use of the Internet after he was 'personally attacked and criticised' by Tamim. A week before the row, the police chief said the Information Ministry and the police, rather than Etisalat, should be authorised to issue Internet licences, as it was their job to monitor information coming into the country and to maintain social and political security. He said Etisalat should only be authorised to connect lines once applications have been cleared by the Ministry and police. (Reuter)

UNITED KINGDOM

It was announced on 6 May that the government will introduce a Bill in November to give the police new powers to enter private property and plant bugging devices against targeted criminals. The aim is to put covert surveillance by the police on a similar basis as MI5 who, after the Security Services Bill becomes law later this year, will be able, with a warrant from the home secretary, to break into and search homes, copy documents, and plant listening devices and cameras without the knowledge of the owners. (*Guardian, Independent*)

During the final stages of a debate on the Armed Forces Bill on 10 May, MPs voted by 188 votes to 120 to uphold the ban on homosexuals in the armed services. (*The Times*)

On 16 May Unipalm Pipex, the biggest provider of Internet access to businesses in the UK, acceded to government pressure by agreeing to censor Internet sites in order to restrict access to pornographic material and other 'unsuitable' sites. A spokesman for Pipex described the move as common sense rather than censorship: 'There will not be access for those sites considered beyond public acceptance... We should set the standards... rather than have standards forced on us.' (*Computing, Independent, Financial Times*)

The video release of Oliver Stone's *Natural Born Killers* was suspended indefinitely on 16 May by its distributors, Warner Home Video. Warner said that in the light of massacres at Dunblane and in Tasmania, its release on video would be 'inappropriate'. (*Guardian, Independent*)

According to the annual report on the Interception of Communications Act, published on 7 June, government ministers author-ised a record number of telephone taps in 1995. Michael Howard, the home secretary, and Michael Forsyth, the Scottish secretary, approved more than 1,000 warrants — some for more than one telephone — at the

request of the security and intelligence agencies. (*Guardian*)

Following his conviction on charges relating to a book on growing cannabis, **Michael Harlow** (*Index* 3/1996) was informed on 16 June that he has been denied legal aid to enable him to appeal against his one-year sentence. The judge at the original trial ordered all copies of the book to be burnt. (PEN)

Parliament voted on 24 June to overturn a provision in the 1689 Bill of Rights, which will make it easier for MPs to sue newspapers over reports of their activities in Parliament. Under the rules of parliamentary privilege, courts were not able to inquire into anything an MP said or did in Parliament, even at the request of an MP. (*Guardian*)

URUGUAY

Federico Fasano, editor-in-chief of the Montevideo daily *La República*, and **Carlo Fasano**, the paper's managing director, were arrested on 23 May on charges brought against them by Paraguay's president Juan Carlos Wasmosy. The two were summarily sentenced to two years in jail for 'insulting the honour of a foreign head of state' in an article on Wasmosy's alleged involve-ment in corruption in the building of the Itaipu dam on the border between Paraguay and Brazil. The defendants were not allowed to present evidence of the truth of the allegations. **Pedro Casadede-munt** and **Ricardo Canese**,

two reporters with *La República*, were also subsequently taken into custody. (IAPA)

Three pirate community radio stations — **El Puente FM, FM Alternativa** and **Emisora de la Villa** — were raided by National Communications Agency staff on 16 June. The three stations, whose signal is too weak for them to be covered by existing regulations, are asking for their legal status to be recognised by the Agency. (AMARC)

USA

Jose Saavedra, a student at the University of Texas in El Paso, has become the first person to be charged for making threats against a public official on the Internet. Saavedra has been charged under anti-terrorism legislation for posting threatening comments about California Senator Tim Leslie on an environmental discussion group. Saavedra faces a fine of US$5,000 and a maximum of three years in jail. (*Guardian*)

On 3 May the Supreme Court agreed to hear a Georgia prisoner's challenge to a new law limiting the right of appeals for death row prisoners. (*International Herald Tribune*)

The Supreme Court ruled against a Baltimore law banning the advertising of alcohol in public places on 20 May. The law was adopted by Baltimore in an attempt to limit under-age drinking and was successfully challenged by brewers Anheuser Busch and the Association of National Advertisers. (Reuter)

On 5 June President Clinton gave backing to legislation which would make church-burning a federal crime. Clinton said there was no evidence of a 'national conspiracy' in the 30 church-burnings that have occurred since 1995 across the American South, but said that clearly 'racial hostility is the driving force behind these incidents'. (*Independent*, *The Times*)

Three federal judges ruled that the online indecency provisions of the Telecommunications Act (*Index* 2/1996, 3/1996) violated the First Amendment and were therefore 'constitutionally intolerable' on 12 June. The panel drew a clear distinction between 'passive' information sources such as television, for which some censorship has been allowed, and 'participatory' sources like the Internet. (*International Herald Tribune*, Reuter)

University professor Daniel Bernstein has been allowed by a federal judge to proceed in his lawsuit challenging the US government's right to control complex encryption technology. The action, which is being sponsored by the Electronic Freedom Foundation, would give Bernstein the right to export encryption software he has developed to colleagues overseas. The US government seeks to control encryption technology because it interferes with the monitoring of communications by the security services. Financial institutions

are also interested in encryption technology as it allows the development of secure international commercial transactions over the Internet. (Reuter)

UZBEKISTAN

On 4 June President Karimov signed a decree pardoning 85 prisoners, of whom 10 were held for their political views, including **Mukhammad Salikh Rashid Bekzhan**, the brother of the leader of the banned **Erk** party, and a senior lecturer from Tashkent Pedagogical Institute, **Abdulla Abdurazzakov**. Some sources suggest that the amnesty was intended to stave off criticism prior to President Karimov's visit to the USA in late June. (AI)

A Human Rights Watch report on Uzbekistan has found that while arrests, detentions and beatings of political dissidents 'have decreased markedly, fundamental civil liberties remain suspended'. Surveillance of individuals and media censorship, says Human Rights Watch, are still commonplace. The report also expresses particular concern over measures taken against members of the country's Islamic community. (HRW)

Recent publication: *Persistent Human Rights Violations and Prospects for Improvement* (HRW/Helsinki, May 1996, 43pp)

VIETNAM

On 19 April the Vietnamese government barred journalists

from covering the return by sea of 317 'boat people' from Malaysia. A Foreign Ministry official said that there had 'not been enough time' to make arrangements for media coverage. (Reuter)

On 18 June the official Voice of Vietnam radio station accused expatriate Vietnamese newspapers and magazines of publishing 'distorted, slanderous and provocative' articles on the eve of the Communist Party congress. The station said the country's achievements were resented by those who played no part in realising them, and that people who said there is no freedom of expression in Vietnam are 'reactionaries'. (SWB)

YEMEN

Riot police broke up demonstrations in Mukalla, Hadhramaut province, in early June after the prosecutor in a rape case referred to all the women in the province as 'prostitutes'. One person was killed and seven injured. **Fouad Bamutrif**, editor of *al-Sharara* newspaper, mouthpiece of the Yemen Socialist Party, was detained briefly. Other journalists who have reported on the situation now say they feel threatened, and there is particular concern for the safety of the Hadhramaut correspondents of the newspaper *al-Ayyam*. On 10 June police fired at a group of protesters outside the government building in Mukalla, wounding at least 10 people. Interior minister Hussein Mohammad Arab and other officials were inside the building at the time, on a visit

NGUYEN CHI THIEN

Poems from the Hanoi Hilton

'For me, poetry is a way of describing the Communist world and commenting on its theories, indirectly. After living under a totalitarian system like Communism we understand very well the phrase 'the pen is mightier than the sword'. Everyone in Vietnam likes poetry for this reason, because of its message.

In February 1966 I was arrested for having written 'reactionary poetry'. I was inside concentration or hard labour camps for the next 11-and-a-half years. For up to nine months at a time I was kept fettered by the leg, alone in a dark cell. At first I wanted to write novels but I realised this would be impossible, so I changed to poetry. I memorised 400 poems in all.

After I was released in July 1977 I managed to distract the attention of the police who were watching me, and went to Hanoi from Haiphong by bus. In three days and nights I put all my poems down on paper. I hid the manuscript and returned to Haiphong without being stopped (the police were visiting me four times a week at that point). I was hoping to get the manuscript to the French embassy on 14 July, but when I got to Hanoi again, the embassy was too well guarded.

In the end, the only embassy I could gain access to was the British one. Three Vietnamese security officials saw me but I rushed in past the guards and came to a halt at a table, which I knocked over in my haste. This succeeded in getting the attention of the diplomats and I handed over to one of them the manuscript, a covering letter and three photographs of myself and my family (see *Index* 3/1982, 'Smuggled Poems'). I asked if I could stay in the building but he said I couldn't as the building was already surrounded. I was escorted from the embassy, barefoot, as my sandals had come off in the hubbub, and 10 policemen arrested me immediately. They taunted me that I would be staying at the 'Hanoi Hilton'. They said they would leave me to die a slow death in there.

As you can see from the photo on the cover of my second volume of poetry, I had negotiations with the security officer in the office of my concentration camp. I suppose this was in response to the growing pressure from organisations and individuals outside the camp and around the world. I believed something might be going on but I had no evidence of it. I learnt later about the joint appeals and the hundreds of letters from all over the world, which had been sent to the authorities. Even after my release in October 1991, I was still kept under very close surveillance until I was permitted to travel abroad. Now I have another 400 poems which I have memorised to put down and print.'

Interviewed by staff of International PEN
Nguyen Chi Thien *spent a total of 27 years in various camps and jails for writing poems considered to be anti-Socialist. His second volume of poetry,* Hoa Dia Nguc Tap 2 *(Flowers from Hell, Volume 2) was published this year in the USA, in Vietnamese only. For an English-language edition, please contact +1 408 736 8774*

to investigate the previous week's events. (Reuter, IFJ)

ZAIRE

A Rwanda-based French freelance journalist, **Adrian De Mun**, was arrested in Goma in mid-May on undisclosed charges. He was transferred to Kinshasa on 23 May. The arrest followed the imposition of a ban on all western journalists travelling to eastern Zaire from neighbouring countries. They are only permitted to reach the region by travelling through Kinshasa. (CPJ)

ZAMBIA

On 30 May the offices of the state-owned *Times of Zambia* were slightly damaged by a bomb explosion. The blast followed several threats to newspaper staff by Black Mamba, a guerrilla group associated with former president Kenneth Kaunda. (CPJ, MISA, Inter Press Service)

On 3 June the *Post* claimed that three of its senior employees have been named as persons targeted for surveillance and eventual assassination by secret intelligence police. The journalists were singled out for their potential to cause 'chaos and public alarm', the paper said. The hit list is also alleged to contain the names of civic activist **Sakwiwa Sikota**,

freelance columnist **Lucy Sichone**, former president **Kenneth Kaunda** and human rights lawyer **Rodger Chongwe**. Home affairs minister Chitalu Sampa has denied the newspaper's allegations. (MISA)

Lawyers for the *Post*'s editor-in-chief, **Fred M'membe**, have said that he will not appear before Parliament to hear the final ruling in a contempt of Parliament charge (*Index* 3/1996). Instead, M'membe is filing an appeal against the ruling, which relates to articles reporting on comments made in Parliament on 30 January 1995 by vice-president Godfrey Miyanda. (MISA)

Bright Mwape and **Chilombo Mwondela** of the *Post* and **Nkonkomalimba Kafunda** and **Anthony Mukwita** of the *Chronicle* were summoned before a legal tribunal on 19 June and ordered to reveal their sources for articles which alleged that legal affairs minister Remmy Mushota had attempted to cash a government cheque for US$166,000. Mushota has also brought criminal defamation charges against the *Post*'s editor, **Fred M'membe**, columnist **Lucy Sichone**, special projects editor **Masautso Phiri** and human rights lawyer **Rodger Chongwe** for writing and commenting on the allegations. (MISA)

ZIMBABWE

An amendment to the Zimbabwe Mass Media Trust's deed was made on 29 April, giving the state the authority to oversee operations. The government has subsequently assumed direct control of the Trust, which owns Zimbabwe's biggest-selling dailies, the Zimbabwe Inter-Africa News Agency and four weekly newspapers. It is anticipated that the approval of the president and the telecommunications minister will now be required in making editorial appointments. (MISA)

★★★

General publications: *Amnesty International Report 1996* (AI, 1996, 360pp); *Reporters Sans Frontières 1996 Report — Freedom of the Press Throughout the World* (RSF, 1996, 380pp); *Arab Constitutional Guarantees of Civil and Political Rights — A Comparative Analysis* by Fateh S Azzam (Cairo Institute for Human Rights Studies, 1996, 134pp)

★★★

Compiled by: Anna Feldman, Kate Thal (Africa); Kate Cooper, Dagmar Schlüter, James Solomon (Americas); Nicholas McAulay, Mansoor Mirza, Sarah Smith, Saul Venit (Asia); Laura Bruni, Robin Jones, Vera Rich (eastern Europe and CIS); Michaela Becker, Philippa Nugent (Middle East); Ian Franklin (western Europe)

INDEX online HTTP://WWW.ONEWORLD.ORG/INDEX_OC/

God is not dead

Turn of the century rationalists pronounced it dead; scientists challenged its incontravertible truths; evolutionists exploded its creation myths. Religion was doomed to rapid eclipse. Yet the turn of the millennium has witnessed a staggering resurgence of belief. Mountains may not move, but the words of new prophets expounding extremes of faith are mobilising masses

(Left) On the walls of Jerusalem: capital of faiths and conflicts

JOHN TUSA

They say God is dead. Why won't He lie down?

NIETZSCHE pronounced it dead; Marx derided it as delusion; Freud regarded it as immature delusion. Scientists dismissed it as unverifiable fantasy; humanists as evasion of grown-up confrontation with life. Religion should, on these terms, have had little or no part to play in the life of the late twentieth century. A belief in Progress now replaced a belief in Paradise tomorrow. Science could prove that the 'answers' offered by religion were untrue, and that faith could not move mountains, nor would mountains come even to latter-day Mohammeds. God's protection was conspicuous by its absence in the trenches of the Somme, in the gas ovens of the Nazi extermination camps, and in a score of other twentieth-century atrocities. Jesus might have told his disciples to 'suffer the little children to come unto me' but, in our more enlightened times, the emphasis seemed to be more on the suffering and not on the protective embrace offered by the Saviour. With such a comprehensive charge sheet against religion, it is remarkable that it did not simply bow to the superior wisdom and experience of the twentieth century and retire with good grace to the museums and history books.

In the event, religion has survived and more than held its own against its critics, many of whom sound positively bad tempered that it continues to offer an alternative set of explanations for human life and behaviour. Even a devout man of religion, the Chief Rabbi of the United Hebrew Congregation of the Commonwealth, Dr Jonathan Sacks, acknowledges as much: 'I don't think there would have been a single social observer in the year 1900 who would have predicted that religion and religions would be as strong in the world today and, indeed, even in the liberal West, as they are. There was a very widespread belief born in the nineteenth century and carried right through to the 1960s that the great world religions were destined for a very rapid eclipse. Now that has not happened and I think that the strength of religion at the end of the century is one of the surprising phenomena of our time.'

So why have religion, faith, religious ritual and observance survived? In part because the answers offered by rationality, scientific progress, and materialism have themselves been tested against their claims and found wanting. If scientific socialism produced Stalin, Mao and all their works, then it said little for either science or socialism. If science produced a world of nuclear weapons where total destruction seemed a distinct possibility, then perhaps science and its followers needed an injection of the values they derided in religion. If secular states were deemed so superior to religious ones, what sort of advertisement for this proposition was Nazi Germany? As Dr Sacks has noted: 'What people are beginning to realise is that you can't predicate salvation in the secular state without offering an intolerable number of human sacrifices. Bad things happen when we deify purely human constructs. Whenever we take one thing, particularly a human artefact, and say that must dominate all else, then we are into idolatry and idolatry always ends in the shedding of human blood...'

The great liberal, Catholic theologian Hans Kung has another, perhaps connected, explanation, as he observes a world where new depths of human behaviour are plumbed regularly, and where religion cannot be blamed for the evils committed. Paradoxically, according to Hans Kung, Nietzsche was right about religion but only if you give his full quotation on the question of God's death. 'Friedrich Nietzsche was very right, saying that if you proclaimed the death of God, then you are by nature tending towards nihilism. So that we have a great deal of practical nihilism today, especially many young people do not know any more what is good and what is bad. We even have children killing children. We have much more suicide among children than in earlier times. All these are what happens if these children have no education in what is ethical and what is the meaning of life.' The 'death of God' was, therefore, no solution; it merely created a new — and possibly far worse — set of moral problems.

Without a religious ingredient to ethical teaching, any evil behaviour is possible; individual self-restraint has been rejected as intolerably restrictive; endless self-gratification has been elevated to a way of life where 'Me First' means everybody else nowhere. No wonder that many find the teachings of personal and social responsibility, consideration for others, selflessness that the world's great religions all provide infinitely preferable to the commercially driven nostrums of modern materialism. And for many, such as Eli Cohen, a Hassidic fundamentalist Jew living in Crown Heights, Brooklyn, materialism fails to offer a full explanation of the world around us. 'There's an essential difference between a view of the world which says that what we see is what is, and one which says that there is some more that we don't see, that is deep, call it spiritual, call it the non-material aspect, metaphysical, any word that you want. I think that the essential belief of the twentieth century is, as we say in computers, "what you see is what you get"; the world view is "what you see is what is", and what you don't see and what you can't measure, is not. The best explanation to what we observe around us is that there is a design — someone or something put it there, and with a purpose that we somehow could identify. That is belief and faith.'

After all, as Hans Kung observes: 'After a certain period of enthusiasm for science, even scientists see that science has its limits, chemistry has its limits, biology cannot explain everything.' Of course, it does not follow that those who reject science as the answer to everything can find the answers of religion any more palatable; but science joins religion in the same category, as a set of beliefs which can no longer claim to offer 'the answer' to the meaning of life.

For many, however, religion has done better than that; it has stood the test of the ghastly experiences of the century. Whether Catholics in Poland under Communism, western hostages in Lebanon at the hands of Islamic fundamentalists, or Christians of many kinds groaning under the multiple oppressions of apartheid in South Africa, God was there, spurring the Church to act effectively in its role of prophetic witness. But God was not easily summoned up on these occasions like some obliging Aladdin. South Africa's Christians were put to the supreme test of faith, that of doubt in God's very presence, as Archbishop Desmond Tutu discovered when, faced with the unbelievable atrocity of the murder of Steve Biko, Tutu cried aloud: 'Is God here at all?' He found his answer: 'It was the natural reaction to seeing evil on the rampage and appearing to be triumphant; a little bit of the cry of dereliction on the cross, but knowing that in the heart of it, in the darkness, it was going to be all right. As Julian of Norwich would say, "All manner of things shall be well."' And this is

Archbishop Desmond Tutu: the faith that moved the might of apartheid

not just a facile optimism; it is hope, hope that says the evidence, the circumstances seem to conspire to say the opposite; but I know in whom I have believed, and if God be for us, who can be against us?'

Few are blessed with that sort of faith, that sort of experience, that sort of result. If God's hand was seen anywhere, it might reasonably be claimed that He — as in the Old Testament — softened the hardened hearts of the tormentors of His people. Most would assert that politics or economics wrought the change in South Africa; others would claim that there was a change of heart in that country and God's hand is as likely an explanation for that transformation as any. Be that as it may, the numbers of people who believe that God had touched their lives and changed them is significant and cannot be rejected as of no account. For them, religion succeeded where humanist-based politics had totally failed.

None of this is to say that the great religions in their traditional forms are as they were even 50 years ago. All are subject to change and evolution. As George Steiner, the critic and philosopher, has observed, there is belief but of an incredibly variegated and diverse kind: 'When I meet, and it is very rare, a consequent atheist, very rare, you have to have enormous discipline, scruple, inner toughness, to be consequent, then hats off! This is somebody who has marched into the tunnel, possibly through it, and is now living a very cold emptiness of what perhaps Freud would call "being grown-up", being adult in some final sense. When I meet a fundamentalist, I may be frightened as hell that he will blow my brains out, but I know what he's on about, I know that his fanaticism or his orthodoxy are a coherent vision of the world. But the enormous mass of us are in a kind of supermarket, a limitless supermarket, shopping a little bit here, a little bit there, a touch of psychoanalysis over here, there is the counter where Nietzsche is selling "God is dead", there until very recently was Marx selling a little bit of social justice at a terrible price. We comparison shop, we run with our trolley from one to the other and there is absolutely no coherent investment of a unified vision of any kind.' But the search for such a coherent vision goes on, a search indistinguishable for many from a search for religious understanding and belief.

It all depends on how you think the circumstances of life can be explained. For Patrick Collinson, Regius professor of religion at Cambridge University, the fact that religious belief is fragmented as never before does not signal its end. 'It's much harder, I think, to imagine a situation so secular as to dispense with that altogether, where everybody's actions, everybody's daily agenda, everybody's hopes and strategies are wholly rational and functional, and everything is done because when you turn on the tap, you know that water will come out of it. I don't think we shall ever live in such a world, whether we should want to, I don't know, but I think we shall, in fact, depend upon an understanding of things which is, if you like, irrational and mythical and, in all sorts of ways, explanatory, and that is broadly religious.'

If religion, the search for something bigger and better than ourselves is so widespread, it may well be because the delights of the material no longer feel so beguiling, the solutions of rationalism and science look less like answers and more like new problems. It may be, too, that many look at the fundamental teachings and experience of the great religions and find them relevant and appealing. In the case of Christianity, these would include selflessness, self-sacrifice, humility, forgiveness and pity to name but a few. In the kind of world that we see around us, no wonder that these have a fresh resonance and relevance. How did we ever do without them? ❏

John Tusa wrote and presented the recent BBC Radio 4 series '20/20: A View of the Century'

DARRYL PINCKNEY

Menacing normality

Extremism is built into the very heart of America's dearest institutions — the Constitution, the Union and the Church. It is the extremes of the mainstream we have most to fear

I USE extremism as a political term. If you chose to become a Trappist monk, I might say that you were taking the religious life to an extreme, but I would see the choice as a matter of individual conscience. If you taught Madison Grant to your class, I would not fret that students were being exposed to a writer of extremist opinions, because it would depend on the context in which his work was understood, what he was taught for and taught as.

But if you thought that everyone must live as a Trappist, if you believed that certain tracts should be taught and not others, and if you committed yourself to realising these views through deliberate measures, then I would say that you had gone from being extreme to being an extremist. It is the element of coercion that defines extremism.

You have to make up your mind how you want to use a word like extremism in the United States because it will never acquire precision. Meaning becomes confused as soon as you begin to contemplate US history and its strains of idealism and ruthless pragmatism, the contradiction between the right to dissent and the urge to ensure a stable society, the distance between the national mythology and the actual events from which that mythology evolved. For instance, it doesn't mean much to describe the ethnocentrism of English settlers in Virginia in 1622 as an example of extremism, even though their cultural ideology justified such treachery as poisoning the leaders of the Powhatan confederacy during peace negotiations in order to weaken the armed resistance of the indian tribes to settler encroachment on the land. Cultural ideology helped to drive the doctrine of Manifest Destiny in the nineteenth century. As settlers pushed westward, Native Americans were killed or displaced. Though there is a debate as to whether this policy was genocidal in intent or effect or both, we don't label as extremist the elimination of indian rivals, the attempt to obliterate a group deemed to be savages. Maybe we should.

Similarly, we don't think of slaveholders as extremists, even though their cultural ideology cast blacks as inferior beings or denied their humanity altogether, because they conformed to the established social order of their day. We have a hard enough time admitting that our Founding Fathers were restrictive in their application of principles, even though we know that the Constitutional Convention determined, for purposes of taxation, that five slaves equalled three free white people, and that Native American tribes were regarded as foreign nations. We might boast that the original consensus prepared for extremism in political life, but not that it was, in itself, tainted by extremist feeling.

We don't condemn as extremist the exercise of power through elected bodies, however amoral or immoral their pursuit of political goals, because we take it for granted that such bodies have some legitimacy. In 183? South Carolina legislators made it a crime to teach slaves to read and write, but the townspeople of Canterbury, Connecticut, in 1832 seem more like extremists, because they burned down a private school rather than see a black girl educated alongside their daughters. We do not hesitate to brand the mob. It is our own loosely agreed upon standards of what is politically acceptable that are disappointed by the nineteenth-century torch thrower. What the distinction in these historical examples suggests is the relation of extremism to the mainstream — that is, we never think of extremism as mainstream. It is always something flipped out.

Thus, a defender of slavery like John C Calhoun is remembered as an extremist, but mostly because he became an ardent Secessionist. In his case Union sentiment functions as the mainstream he pitched himself to correct. If we wouldn't think of a slaveholder as being extremist, we would think of a defender of the Confederacy as being so — to the extent that he would continue to adhere to the ideology, deny that slavery had been abolished, uphold penal servitude, and seek revenge for the change in the social order. George Custer comes to mind, but we are reared on such romantic images of the South and its lost causes that his extremism as a Confederate general and indian fighter is obscured by his glamour. Even

New Orlean's slave auction 1865: extreme conformity lives on

so, we might feel that Custer had asked for his last stand, because he was on the brink of that time when people ought not to have gone in for indian massacres. We settle unpleasant issues in our national past by saying that people were limited by their cultural moment, but we also have a schedule about when people ought to have known better.

Something about the movement of history, a perhaps overly determined idea of social progress, marks, in retrospect, certain times when people ought to have begun to know better concerning questions of social tolerance and political equality. Extremism, in this view, becomes a reaction, an allegiance to the outdated, the obsolete, an angry, false nostalgia, a hard, bitter refusal. That is why extremism always seems to be an offence of the right wing. Because as social beings we live with a sense of when the time has come in which people ought to know better, because we measure our national self in relation to our past national self, we do not put extremists of the left in the same category as extremists of the right. In fact, we don't call radical progressives in US history extremists at all.

Harriet Beecher Stowe as a Swedenborgian Christian was way out there, but because she was on the side of abolitionism we think of her as militant. We skip over the details of John Brown's bloody raid as one of the grim opening chapters of the Civil War, because he, too, was on abolition's side. Had John Brown been a forerunner of the white-hooded night riders, we would recall him as a stone-cold extremist, not as a misguided leader of a doomed insurrection. If we think of the extremist as not part of the mainstream, we think of the militant as powerless. The Black Panthers of the 1960s were seen to threaten the established order by publicly announcing themselves as armed black men, but the power in the ensuing confrontations was always with the FBI and the local police forces. Militants we think of as having a point about injustice or oppression. Extremists we think of as having only a point of view. Militants don't have power, they have influence. The test is that militants can make you feel guilty, but extremists can't.

If you belong to the right wing, then your whole attitude to history is different. Whatever you claim to feel as a burning fire demands expression as an absolute in order to be convincing. This is the appeal of the Christian Right, that broad banner under which extremist souls in the US are now converging. The Christian Right appears to be in the tradition that allowed religious movements in the US to flourish, a tradition very much alive, which explains the depths of live-and-let-live sympathy for most contemporary cults and alternative churches, so long as they are not next door. But that tradition, begun before the mass migration of the European poor to the US in the second half of the nineteenth century, in which America is seemingly populated by every shade of Anabaptist, is too passive for the Christian Right. The American descendants of the 'Bolsheviks of the Reformation' had joined movements of renunciation. They wanted to come to the New World and then they wanted to be left alone. Not every cult is politically extremist and the feature of these cults is that they are closed and have a doctrine that you have to sign up to in a comprehensive way. Cult members have committed a kind of psychic suicide and are just trying to get through the rest of their lives. They are people who want less responsibility as citizens, not more. If you belong to the Christian Right, however, you would claim a tradition of religious liberty simply as an ennobling precedent for whatever it is you have up your sleeve.

The Christian Right is firmly in another American religious tradition, that of extremists as lovers of conformity. The Puritan leaders of the Massachusetts Bay Colony distrusted Anne Hutchinson's influence among worshippers and banished her in 1638. Mrs Hutchinson, the fanatical Calvinist, believed that God spoke directly to her and that she therefore obeyed a power greater than that of the ministers who cherished their civil authority more than they did their covenant with God, a civil authority that permitted them to burn witches and hang Quakers in the name of orthodoxy. Similarly, the Mormons met with suspicion up until Utah won statehood in 1890. After the church fathers had cleaned up their act enough for Washington's acceptance, they busily persecuted their own heretics. Today, the City on a Hill is no less a political capital and the Christian Right seems to be saying that all those who enter through these gates must be White Like Me.

The Christian Right is a movement of resentment, which makes it available to extremist manipulation. What the Christian Right resents is not the tyranny of liberals in office or positions of cultural influence. Anyone with an honest recollection of the Vietnam War era knows that political correctness did not originate as a sin of the left. That was at a time when you were bullied by teachers and fellow students to pray and then to recite the Pledge of Allegiance. What the Christian Right resents is the intellectual prestige of certain liberal ideas, the moral and ethical persuasiveness of liberal social hopes. This would seem to include the provision in the US social contract that called for separation of church and state, the very article on which their unhindered existence depends. The libertarian rhetoric of the Christian Right is a cloaking device because the individualism they pretend to be protecting is conformist, anti-communal, especially now that there are some 650 mosques nationwide and only one third of the followers of Islam in the US are African American.

This rhetoric becomes political in character through the effort to translate religious belief into civil law. Someone on the Christian Right doesn't believe that secularism has gone too far, he or she fears that change has gone too far. The US federal government is the agency responsible for the enforcement of, say, affirmative action regulations or, earlier, desegregation orders. That is why conservatives in the US are most often found in the ranks of states' rights proponents, because they can more effectively obstruct change on the local level, free of interfering directives from the Washington bureaucracy. The Christian Right is pro-individual and anti-central government in its rhetoric mostly because its followers

Louis Farrakhan, Nation of Islam: blackness past its sell-by date

feel that they have lost control of that government. That is why they assert
that they represent majority feeling, which is itself a perversion, because

the classic definition of democracy is not majority rule, but the protection of minorities.

Not everyone on the Christian Right is also a member of the National Rifle Association, the Minutemen, or the Michigan Militia. They don't have to be. In the US the racist or the extremist is always depicted in film or on television as a grotesque, so that people sitting in the dark can reassure themselves that that isn't them. They file out dressed in the robes of the mainstream. But extremist groups share some of the frustrations of the Christian Right: were the federal government still committed to segregation perhaps there would have been no separatists holed up in that Montana farmhouse. We think of the Ku Klux Klan as selecting isolated black sharecroppers as victims, when, historically, they took aim at blacks who had done too well in business. Some of the recent arson attacks on black churches in the South may well prove to have been motivated more by land-grabbing greed than race hate, which has a racist component in that whites often demonstrate that if a black does too well then being white seems to lose something of its value. There is something of fear of being devalued as whites in the resentment of the Christian Right. They have their inadvertent allies, among them Farrakhan, who seeks to profit from a concept of blackness that is just as artificial and past its sell-by date as whiteness.

You get the feeling that after the Iran hostage crisis in 1979, the Christian Right decided that uncompromising fundamentalism worked as a strategy, that the theocratic mood could salvage the social construct of whiteness, in the way that anti-abortion activists on the Christian Right adopted the civil disobedience tactics of the Civil Rights era, except that no civil rights worker ever shot Bull Connor or any other sheriff who brought dogs to demonstrations, whereas pro-life extremists are not above gunning down doctors outside clinics. You get the feeling that the Christian Right would recognise the satisfaction in the Maoist slogan: 'The world is in chaos. Situation excellent.'

If the Christian Right did not reawaken the country's pride in its millenarian streak, it is basking in it. It is said that in the last days of the earth the pages of every copy of the Quran will go blank. No doubt the Bible will go on talking. A country deserves the extremists it gets. ❑

Darryl Pinckney is author of a novel, High Cotton *(Farrar, Straus & Giroux, 1992), and writes for the* New York Review of Books

ADAM NEWEY

Networking for God

God's minions are marching on the superhighway, banners waving, preachers and zealots to the fore. But is it any more than a (mutually) self-cancelling Tower of Babel effect?

IF ANYTHING deserves to be banned, so the argument goes, it's hate speech. Say what you like about the central importance of freedom of expression in a democratic society, the freedom to peddle ethnic, religious or communal hatred is simply one freedom too many. And when it comes to particular types of expression — denying the Holocaust, for example, or directly inciting violence against people of other races or faiths — the outrage inspired is especially and understandably intense.

These concerns about hate speech are by no means new. But with the arrival of the Internet, and no apparent end in sight to its spread, the issues have taken on a new significance. For here is a group of media in which anyone, in theory, can participate (the old stricture about freedom of the press only being important if you happen to own one, doesn't apply). Here too are media in which, if you know where to look, you can find some extremely vicious forms of bigotry. Furthermore, as the recent debacle in the US over the Communications Decency Act shows, these media are going to be very resistant to statutory regulation. Nonetheless the calls for regulation are growing, as evidenced by an important paper published in April by the London-based Institute for Jewish Policy Research, entitled *The Governance of Cyberspace*.

But what the old arguments for regulation haven't yet taken into account is the fact that the Internet just isn't like any other kind of medium we have ever had. Because it is both interactive and mass-participatory the Internet — and especially the World Wide Web — is much more than a new and cleverer way of moving information around

'The jews who troll the usenet constantly crying about anti-semitism have found the Internet a nice way to be able to spew trash that no decent person would ever say to another individual... The perverted overtones of their filth is ingrained in their minds from their religious book, the Talmud, which is full of pornographic and indecent material, including a passage which allows jews to have relations with little girls and a passage which allows the rape of 'gentile' women.'

(from Christian Identity Online, http://www.alaska.net:80/~schoedel/)

from one person or place to another. It has begun to take on the contours of a genuine community in its own right, and its culture is strongly libertarian.

If it resembles anything at all, the World Wide Web most resembles Borges' great Library of Babel. This library contains a mind-boggling array of thoughts and words making up practically every conceivable human utterance in every conceivable language. Every nuance, every shade of meaning finds expression there. The library, as a result, may or may not be infinite in size. But where Borges' story is a grand intellectual joke about language and identity, the Web, by blurring many traditional boundaries — not just between texts on a screen but between different political communities — is radically recasting important questions about the connections between language and toleration.

The Web's ability to transport the reader instantly, in mid-sentence if you like, from the page being read to a completely different page, or a completely different computer, in a different part of the world, is what makes it a distinctively new kind of reading medium. In some cases, this can further one's understanding of a subject by bringing out unsuspected, or unstated, connections: much depends on how good the provider of the material is at putting in imaginative and informative links.

For instance, hypertext links can be quite revealing about the loose but complex coalition that makes up America's far right: from a site covering the whole gamut of right-wing issues from prayer in schools and abortion to white supremacy and gun control, one can follow a link to, say, the unashamedly neo-Nazi Stormfront site; and from there one can link to the

> 'Just like a low-lying snake that slithers from dark place to dark place, he spreads his venom to innocent victims. This is David Cole, who takes pride in his demonic occupation: Holocaust denier of the Six Million Jews... After all this Cole mania that the media have played on, don't you think it's time that we flush this rotten, sick individual down the toilet, where the rest of the waste lies? One less David Cole in the world will certainly not end Jew-hatred, but it will have removed a dangerous parasitic, disease-ridden bacteria from infecting society.'
>
> *(from the Jewish Defense League, http://www.jdl.org/)*

official Pat Buchanan homepage, replete with extracts from his homilies on family, faith and freedom. What this reveals about Buchanan's political appeal needs no elucidation. What's important, though, is that absolute freedom of access to such a powerful communications network is almost certainly allowing the far right to organise among themselves, both in the US and internationally, as never before. And it certainly allows them to reach — and therefore offend — more people than they ever could. So, aren't these good reasons for regulating the Web?

Again, it's important to remember how new and how different this medium is. There's something ironic in the fact that America's religious right should have taken so strongly to the Web. Admittedly, some evangelical Christians believe that the digital communications revolution,

> 'You are wicked deceivers of the American people. You have sucked their blood. You are not real Jews, those of you that are not real Jews. You are of the synagogue of Satan, and you have wrapped your tentacles around the US government and you are deceiving and sending this nation to hell. But I warn you in the Name of Allah, you would be wise to leave me alone. But if you choose to crucify me, know that Allah will crucify you.'
>
> *(from The Nation of Islam Online, http://www.noi.org/)*

by helping to spread God's word through all corners of the world, is helping to speed the arrival of the endtimes foretold in the book of Revelation. But as a medium and as a community, the Web represents par excellence everything that is anathema to the religious right: a post-modern nightmare come true, in which no authority exists to guide the reader towards truth and away from falsity, in which each user is free to make whatever sense and take whatever value they can from the material they find. Evolution can exist alongside creationism, gay activism alongside diatribes against the sin of Sodom, diametrical opposites occupying the same, undifferentiated virtual space.

Part of the appeal of the most intolerant forms of religious militancy is that they offer an authoritative cultural, moral and spiritual standpoint from which other, competing standpoints can be judged. The believer's sense of identity is strengthened by the fact that the belief is based on the exclusion of others. What the Web offers, on the other hand, is nothing more than the chance to take one's place among the bazaar of exotic goods on display to an endlessly shifting group of consumers. Unless they are grabbed straight away by what they see, readers tend not to hang around — they just follow the nearest link

Stormfront homepage

elsewhere. And, for many users, identity can inhere as much in belonging to the wider community of net users — being a 'netizen' in the jargon — as belonging to any narrow group of religious, political or cultural activists who just happen to be online.

This is one reason why the Web is perhaps as close as we have ever come to creating a true market-place of ideas. What has mainly prevented the market-place of ideas operating in other media is that the real, economic, market always intrudes to skew it in favour of some (profitable) forms of expression over others. Not so with the Internet, at least not while access is relatively cheap and while anything goes in terms of content. Any public medium thatcan carry, without prejudice, speeches by

> 'Proper racial pride is important. You are what you are, and cannot change your racial background. Make the most of it as a Christian! Christian values must come first! Also Christian charity. We will help Negroes get back in touch with their culture; they will be sent on a journey back to their roots — Africa. Also Arabs and Asians will be repatriated to the lands of their ancestors... American Indians will be allowed to stay. Latins and Mexican-Americans, if not illegally here, will also be allowed to stay.'
>
> *(from RG Thatcher's Proposal for American Political Reform,*
> *http://www.alaska.net/~schoedel/thatcher/proposal.html)*

Louis Farrakhan, material from the Jewish Defense League and Biblical justifications for white supremacy, is a remarkable medium indeed.

In the end, it is this all-inclusive nature that prevents the Web from being an effective vehicle for intolerance. The poisonous bigotry simply gets lost among the rest of the cyberbabble, its ability to influence as propaganda severely weakened by its proximity to opposing and incompatible bigotries. If Goebbels had had the opportunity of using the Web, he would still have chosen film as a far more effective propaganda tool.

The virtual space of the Internet, by contrast, in which geographies are blurred, customs undermined and norms challenged, is in itself a metaphor for a tolerant, self-regulating human community, in which

> 'Eugenics must be practised in selecting a mate for marriage. Also people who have serious genetic problems in their families should be sterilised. These people, if they wish to have children, should adopt them. The children they adopt must be of their own race... We will send the Jews in a mass exodus to the land of Palestine.'
>
> *(from RG Thatcher's Proposal for American Political Reform)*

religious, political and tribal divisions can at least be addressed and acknowledged, if not necessarily overcome. The activists of the Jewish Defense League will continue to use it to publicise their well-argued position for limits on far-right expression on the Internet (alongside their own forms of hate speech); the far right will continue to be zealous in claiming their full and unfettered rights to freedom of speech. But as long as that conversation is going on, things can't be going too badly.

In his ruling against the Communications Decency Act (CDA) on 12 June, US District Court Judge Stewart Dalzell said: 'As the most participatory form of mass speech yet developed, the Internet deserves the highest protection from government intrusion... Just as the strength of the Internet is chaos, so the strength of our liberty depends upon the chaos and cacophony of the unfettered speech the First Amendment protects.'

> 'There is either an Israel or a 'Palestine': there cannot be both. Since there is no 'Palestinian' land there no 'Palestinian' people, either. Therefore there is no land to take away from them since they have absolutely no title or claim to any of it; it belongs solely to the Jewish people because God gave it to us... Do normal Jews owe the 'Palestinians' anything? Yes we do. We owe it to them to let them know that we intend to continue living in our land, even at the cost of their lives.'
>
> *(from Lord Zion's Homepage, http://ryker.itech.cup.edu/~gseese/)*

The arrival, this summer, of the Platform for Internet Content Selection (PICS) to enable regulation by the user at the point of delivery (a kind of v-chip for the Internet) seems at the moment to offer the best chance of averting further statutory measures. The CDA, by slamming down the shutters at the first sight of the undesirable, was nothing more than a crude attempt to foreclose on the future. The Internet may be neither promised land nor rediscovered Eden, but it is very probably the way of all our futures. As we go surfing into the millennium, we can shut our eyes and pretend it isn't happening — or we can embrace the challenge and ride the big wave. ❑

IRENA MARYNIAK

Moscow 1993: Orthodox missionairies fight back

Never mind the politics, feel the spirit

Religion is all the rage in Russia. Confessions old and new, large and small; New Age cults from abroad as well as the homespun messianic variety are thriving. And with a credibility rating of 53 per cent, the Orthodox Church is well ahead of the presidency, the Communist Party and the army

RUSSIA, a Jungian friend explained to me once, is an *anima* country. Here — psychologically and culturally — emotion, intuition, mysticism and paranoia prevail. In many ways, the sprawling and incoherent shape of Russian life and polity falls far more readily into the domain of clairvoyance than rational analysis.

In the Soviet years, the words 'spirit' and 'soul' were part and parcel of daily ideo-speak, scientific materialism notwithstanding. They referred, generally, to notions of collective consciousness or group persona; it was through the collective, ideologues would say, that you gained spiritual maturity. Now, as the revived Orthodox Church struggles to contain the perennial crop of superstition, pre-Christian animism and shamanistic tradition that survived the Tsars and the Soviet state, religious sectarianism, spiritualism, and sorcery are thriving, enriched by 'techno-speak' and New Age imports from India, Japan, Korea and the USA.

Have faith, then, and fear not. A bent safety pin poised over the architrave of your front door will protect you from the evil eye; if negative bio-energy upsets your aura there's bound to be a freelance healer cum witch or wizard in a block close-by, eager to chant you into health or offer a soothing massage. If business needs a boost, try a graduate from Moscow's school for witches: 'youthful, attractive with good dress sense and a lovely voice'. She'll have paid US$5,000 to train in psychoanalysis, hypnosis, extra-sensory perception, poltergeist removal, tarot cards, dream decoding, herbal healing and prophecy.

Or try a personal astrological chart from famed star-gazer Tamara Globa. A snip at US$500. Her clients include Ruslan Khasbulatov and Vladimir Zhirinovsky, so one hears. You may need to keep a note of that phone number though; spiritual healers are banned from advertising by presidential decree.

Not that Boris Yeltsin has been averse to a little extra-sensory help himself. The first round of the presidential election saw an influential retinue of astrologers and sorcerers delivering warnings of upheaval and bloodshed in the run-up to polling day. The bomb which exploded in the Moscow metro on 11 June will have reinforced their position. The presidential security service, as it stood prior to the recent dismissal of Lt Gen Alexander Korzhakov, had as its deputy Gen Georgy ('Zhora') Rogozin, a former KGB officer widely believed to be a long-standing adept of the occult. Rogozin is also erstwhile chief scientist to the first division of the National Security Institute, where he was reportedly given *carte blanche to* pursue interests which included experiments in telepathic communication and the recovery of information from the departed by brainwave scans taken from the skull. Reports by distinguished Moscow journalists have spoken of the fear and loathing in which this latter-day Merlin is held by a Kremlin elite still terrorised by tapping mechanisms and video cameras. They have drawn pictures of a presidency subsumed to astrological charts, spinning saucers, energy fields, healing sessions and the cabbala. On the political front, Rogozin is also a supporter of the pro-Yeltsin movement 'Reforms: the New Deals', which operates under the slogan 'Democracy, Patriotism, Statehood' and calls for the restoration of the role of the state in the economy and social welfare. His *étatiste* credentials have all but brought sorcery into the mainstream of Russian political culture.

By way of ramification, perhaps, state and military accoutrements are all the rage among the extra-sensory set. Mystic faith-healer Dzhuna Davitashvili is to be seen sporting an army uniform and armed forces badge. She made her name reportedly easing Leonid Brezhnev's declining years. Now she apparently has ties with Boris Yeltsin: 'Businesslike chats,' she says. 'He respects me, I respect him.' Her friends also include Moscow mayor Yuri Luzhkov, and Yeltsin's chief of staff Sergei Filatov. Then there is wizard Yuri Longo, who does televised psychic seances and claims he can bring the dead back to life. His intimates are said to include KGB generals and he has conducted hypnosis seances for the former secret police to help rid them of any lingering bad vibes.

Not to be outdone, the Orthodox Church too is taking a fresh look at exorcism and purveying a new line in soul purification services. Many believers have no qualms about turning to shamans or sorcerers despite the hierarchy's round condemnation of folk medicine, fortune-telling and parapsychology as 'devil worship'.

The surge of support for Orthodox Christianity evident in the early 1990s has been followed by a decline of interest — particularly in attending the lengthy, if majestically beautiful, Church liturgy. An estimated 50 per cent of Russia's population still sees itself as broadly Christian, but polls suggest that those who profess a strictly Orthodox allegiance are likely to take a more positive view than most of the Communist Party and Stalin. They are also less likely to recognise any necessity to protect human rights.

But as a national institution, with a credibility rating of 53 per cent, the

Church is well ahead of the presidency, the Communist Party and the army. That should come as no surprise. For a millennium, Russia's awareness of itself as a nation-state has been sustained by the myth of its identity as a community of 'right believers' or 'right worshippers', for that is the meaning of *pravoslavnyi* — the Russian word for Orthodox Christian. If people feel ambivalent these days about the credentials of a clergy silenced, infiltrated and provoked for seven decades, they are willing to support Orthodoxy as a flagship for their national identity, and as the sole organisation in the country which expresses the historical and moral integration of the state. Rather like the Soviet Communist Party, the Church is a nation-wide club offering a badge, community, social security and support. But the lack of enthusiasm for education, science or cultural development among some traditionalist priests, and teachings on humility, meekness, patience and obedience, do little to endear Orthodox Christianity to potential adherents keen to mow their way into the free market. As a platform for recovering the community spirit and collective self-respect in hard times though, no political party can match it. Alliance with the Patriarch is a way of shoring up moral credibility for Communist, nationalist and reformer alike. The newly appointed security chief, Gen Alexander Lebed, shares a platform with churchmen; Vladimir Zhirinovsky, Viktor Chernomyrdin and Gennady Zyuganov are all seen hobnobbing with hierarchs. The new Communist Party has reaffirmed the pre-revolutionary primacy of Orthodoxy and of an empire it talks of reuniting 'voluntarily'.

A flood of foreign missionairies, 30,000 strong, is swamping the new 'dark continent' with Bibles, junk publicity...and promises of study trips to the West

The Church has become an umbrella organisation for politicians and parties on the make, although shoots of grass roots religious pluralism remain a source of anxiety. Up to four per cent of the population are estimated to be participating in 'sectarian' activity, with a reported 12,000 religious communes identified in 1996. And then there is that flood of brash foreign missionaries (about 30,000 since the Wall fell) swamping this, the new 'dark continent' of eastern Europe, with Bibles, junk publicity, medical aid, free English-language teaching and promises of study trips to the West.

Summer 1993, which saw the mass baptism of 2,000 Jehovah's

Witnesses in the Locomotive Stadium in Moscow, also signalled the start of the Church's campaign to introduce legislation controlling undesirable religious imports. Since then there have been attempts by clergy in the provinces to introduce police measures to discourage new arrivals, while the Metropolitan of Orenburg tried to rouse local Cossacks to break up rallies held by American Adventists (he was thwarted by the local administration). Reports that missionaries in Atlanta are planning to send delegates to every school in the former USSR have caused intense anxiety. 'Like Africa under colonisation, our country is being viewed as a field for target practice to which they bring their "high culture and enlightenment",' Father Aleksy Moroz, wrote recently in one widely distributed Church pamphlet. 'Vast financial resources are expended to destroy what is left of the Orthodox faith in our hearts, to relegate Russia to spiritual and economic servitude, subjugate it to western influence, impose the West's culture and stereotypical thought, to transform our country into a colony for raw materials, and be a parasite on its natural and human resources.'

Fundamentalist Baptists, Mormons, the Unification Church (which has distributed a promotional textbook called *My World* in 2,000 Russian schools), Hare Krishnas (claiming a following of up to 700,000) and Scientologists (over 12,000 in Moscow alone) are increasingly viewed by the Church and the media as harmful or dangerous. The Japanese cult Aum Shinri Kyo, thought to have been behind the nerve gas attack which killed 12 people and injured 5,000 in the Tokyo subway in March 1995, has 30,000 followers in Russia and assets in excess of US$7 million. Investigations were carried out into Russian involvement in the attack; no evidence was found, but the organisation was suspended. Its leader in Russia, Toshiyasu Onchi, is on bail following charges of threatening public security and citizens' health. The investigation continues.

New religions come in all shapes and sizes: home grown or foreign, some closed and inclined to relieve their followers of homes and possessions while fomenting millenarian paranoia, others more benign. The 'Mother of God' cult, for instance, founded by a monk, indulges in hate rhetoric against all women who fail to repent; while 'Vissarion's Church of the Last Precept', set up by an ex-policeman and now self-styled Messiah, is building an eco-friendly 'Sun City' in the Siberian forest.

There have been some juicy stories too, one centering around the schismatic 'White Brotherhood' which today operates underground in

Russia and Ukraine. Its leaders, Yuri Krivonogov (a former academic interested in mind control who, according to some evidence, was also employed by the KGB) and Marina Tsvigun (once a journalist, who woke up after the last of a series of abortions declaring she was God), succeeded in recruiting up to 7,000 members in three years. Incoherently worded leaflets, distributed throughout the CIS with baffling efficiency, claimed that Tsvigun, or Maria Devi Khristos as she prefers to be known, was the second incarnation of the Christ returned to usher in an Apocalypse scheduled for 14 November 1993. Khristos was to die outside the Cathedral of St Sofia in Kiev in the presence of her followers, and be resurrected with them three days later. Thousands of cult followers, mostly undernourished-looking teenagers, some with anxious parents in tow, flooded the city to await the Last Day. But the unstilled world whirled on: 989 people were arrested; the detained chanted and sang and declared a string of hunger strikes that ran into December; bomb threats were made against government buildings, churches and the Chernobyl nuclear plant; and Krivonogov claimed an arithmetical error. He and Marina were subsequently charged with inciting mass disorder and damaging citizens' health. He was sentenced to seven years' imprisonment, she to four.

The Church's campaign and its attempts to place restrictions on domestic and foreign cults or missions — including well-heeled Protestant denominations — have made international groups bristle. The spectre of religious persecution still hangs over Russia (200,000 priests were killed in the Soviet years and half a million repressed) and religious aid is a source of humanitarian support the Russian government can't sniff at. Restrictive measures are being examined to appease Church clerics, but recent emphasis has been on conciliatory tax concessions for religious groupings. The Communists, meanwhile, appear committed to exposing 'totalitarian sects' and purging the country of unwelcome foreign missionaries. Their rhetoric has been read as signalling planned repressive measures against New Age movements and — although the party has guaranteed religious equality to Orthodox Christians, Old Believers, Muslims and Buddhists — Protestants and Jews seem to have been excluded.

As for the shaven-headed members of the neo-Nazi 'Russian National Unity Party', Yeltsin supporters all, they continue to claim that the swastika is Russia's main religious symbol ('a symbol for kindness') and that their salute is a medieval Russian greeting in which the hand goes up from the heart towards God. ❑

URVASHI BUTALIA

Kali's revenge

SUSHMA SWARAJ was the only woman minister in the Bharatiya Janata Party (BJP) government that came briefly to power after the Indian elections in May. Taking charge of the important Information and Broadcasting Ministry, Swaraj announced that she was concerned at the bad influence of 'western' values on 'Indian' culture; she suggested it was time women newsreaders on television dressed a little more 'decently'.

That the BJP government was short-lived, is no cause for relief. Over the last several years, the

Calcutta workshop: gods in waiting

right has been making consistent gains in electoral politics. One of their most successful strategies has been to mobilise women; in this they have succeeded beyond even their own expectations. The Rashtra Sevika Samiti, the women's wing of the Rashtriya Swayamsevak Sangh (RSS), now has 2,000 members in its Delhi unit. Similar units exist all over India, as do other, similar organisations. Members are drawn from some of the most conservative of backgrounds: middle-class, trader and service-sector families. And in times of violent upheaval, women are now increasingly in evidence.

The right has now also become a real career option for women wishing to make their way in politics. If other parties are reluctant to include women in their ranks (and while most major parties included women's demands in their manifestos, the current Parliament has barely a dozen women in it), the right has gradually begun to open its doors to them. And indeed to use them to establish an image of 'liberalness' and 'secularity'. Swaraj, for example, barring a few occasions, speaks in the seductive language of the liberal middle class which makes her enormously popular.

The implications of this for Indian women are double edged. In some ways, right-wing parties have opened up spaces for women — brought them, as historian Tanika Sarkar says, 'into activist, public roles and thereby increased their bargaining power within their homes, as political activism invariably does to some extent'. But in doing so, women have also, in a sense, tied themselves to the broader political ideology of the right, one which is, in the final analysis, both fascist and patriarchal.

And, as the recent elections have shown, one of the most successful strategies of the right has been to master the skill of presenting itself as both liberal and middle-of-the-road. During its short stint in power, the right-wing government took care to tread a careful middle path in everything — despite its more aggressive rhetoric earlier. It was to this end, too, that women figured prominently in the manifesto of the BJP. The party pegged itself to fight for a uniform civil code, something with which they hoped to win over large numbers of women. At present, in 'personal' matters such as marriage, inheritance, adoption and divorce, women of different communities are governed by different personal laws. What was obscured by the BJP's proposal was that 'uniformity' meant Hindu.

While it has raised the status of its own women, feminists and feminist activists have come in for considerable attack, accused of being 'western', 'not culturally rooted', 'urban' and so on. Such accusations are easy to level and sometimes stick. Sadly, many women's groups have responded by falling into the trap of 'proving' their community or local origins. This has often meant compromise on the issues they are fighting for. For example, groups who would earlier not have compromised at all on the issue of whether or not there should be a uniform system of gender-just laws for women in India are today asserting that such a system should not be imposed from above: communities themselves must be ready for change from within.

The right has consistently appropriated the language of women's rights. Having successfully used the issues of the movement — going into homes and helping sort out cases of domestic violence for example — to draw women into its fold, it is now accusing the movement of being 'alien' and 'foreign'. More recently, its cultivation of a new, more liberal self image has led to women activists being cast as 'strident', 'dogmatic' and more.

Between now and the next election, the right will regroup and prepare to come back stronger than ever. The signs of danger for women are clear; their strategies, too, must be ready.

Urvashi Butalia is a founder of the publishing house Kali for Women, Delhi

BARUCH KIMMERLING

Unholy covenant

Yitzhak Rabin was murdered because his policies threatened the creeping process that is moving Israel away from a secular state to one ruled by religious laws

THE MURDER of Yitzhak Rabin is not the end, nor is it the beginning. This murder is part of a process gaining momentum in Israeli society for reasons built into its fundamental identity. Within this society, two different identity groups are contending. Each identity group possesses its own mutually incompatible internal logic and rules of the game. For the majority of Israel's Jewish population, their coexistence is the source of its constant dilemma: the systemic disorder within the Israeli identity. In the course of the periodic roller-coaster of Israeli schizophrenia, identities rise and fall: now one, now the other is paramount.

One identity, that of the modern society functioning by the accepted laws of developed western societies and based on the concept of citizenship, is usually termed 'civil'. Citizens have obligations and rights that are defined both *vis-à-vis* the state and other citizens. Participation in the collective purports to be voluntary and is expressed by means of an unwritten social contract. Rights and obligations are constitutionally defined in written laws and captured in the accepted norms of civil society at any given time. This is the identity of 'The State of Israel'.

The second identity is the 'tribal-religious', sometimes defined as 'Jewish'. Its political and social goals, as well as the world-view of those individuals and groups who carry this identity — particularly those who carry it in its 'pure' form — are very different from those crystallised by the secular community that originally built this society.

At the risk of over simplifying: selective interpretation of the Jewish *halacha* (religious law) constitutes the definitive source of authority for this sector of the population. Its aim — hidden or disclosed — is the creation of a halachic Jewish state. This is 'The Land of Israel', a place for Jews only and where rights, based on halachic criteria, are accorded strictly in proportion to the ethno-religious purity of their 'Jewishness'. In principle one is born into this group or enters only with great difficulty; converts are seen as sores on the body. 'The Land of Israel' is far more than a territorial concept: it is theological. If 'gentiles' are found within it, the laws applicable to them are, according to the Bible and the *halacha*, those dealt out to the Canaanites, Jebusites and Philistines in ancient times.

Jerusalem 1990: divided in the faith

The deepening split within the 'nation' is dividing it into two 'nations' and no confused rhetoric on 'unity' will help. The territorial conflict, as it were, over control of 'Judea and Samaria' [aka the West Bank] and the battle of 'Gush Emunim' [Block of the Faithful] and their extremist religious allies, conceals a more fundamental battle over political, cultural and religious control throughout Israel. This battle only partially overlaps the battle between right and left, between hawks and doves and between 'militarists' and those who share the aspirations of the 'Peace' movement or the left-wing parties.

Yitzhak Rabin was murdered because his policies threatened the continuing centrality of the tribal or primordial foundations of Israeli society and the creeping process moving Israel towards a Jewish state that would eventually be run according to religious law. Certain religious authorities labelled him a 'traitor' whose death was justified. Anyone who dares to return the state to a civil path, including right-wing politicians, should meet the same fate.

This murder has clarified the urgent need to decide which society we aspire to establish: a halachic — religious — Jewish state, where the masters rule over a Palestinian majority stripped of their basic rights of self-determination; or a democratic state in which not only are religion and state separated, but there is a wall between religion and nationalism.

The failure of Israeli democracy to develop institutions dealing with fundamental problems or even to put such problems on the agenda for public debate, will end in further blood-letting between 'The State of Israel' and 'The Land of Israel'. The first shots were fired at the Cave of the Patriarchs by Baruch Goldstein, the Jewish settler who massacred a group of Muslim worshippers in Hebron — or maybe even earlier when the grenade thrown into a Peace Now rally killed the student Emil Greenzweig — and were followed by the burst of fire cutting down Prime Minister Rabin. The fingers on the triggers were different; the ideological motivation is identical.

The opening shots in a civil war do not necessarily have its partisans rushing to don the uniforms of armies or militias as in the USA, Spain, Lebanon or Yugoslavia. A cultural war is a civil war and its increasing violence is already putting down roots deep into the soil of Israeli society. Whether they recognise it or not, the secular right in Israeli political culture and the 'militarism' of the left, are the tools of religious nationalism and tribalism. They have been dragged along without realising the vast conflict of interests underlying their 'alliance'.

Shorn of its empty rhetoric in the wake of Rabin's assassination, the secular right has still not decided on whose side it will stand in this conflict. A decision is urgent, for its choice will determine how much blood is shed, how much is saved. As long as the secular right lacks a leadership with enough spirit and vision to realise the danger inherent in the present conflict of interest, there is little ground for believing it will prevent the unholy alliance between nationalism and religious fundamentalism. ❏

Baruch Kimmerling is a professor of sociology at the Hebrew University of Jerusalem, Israel. His publications include Palestinians: The Making of a People *(Harvard University Press, 1994) co-authored with Joel Migdal. This column, translated by Debbie Perla, first appeared in* Ha'aretz, *8 November 1995*

JEWISH DEFENCE LEAGUE...
"KAHANE CHAI"
A WARNING TO THE "MUSLIM" COMMUNITY:-
NO MORE WILL BE ISSUED:-

TO THOSE THAT HAVE SEEN OUR STRENGTH AND OUR SENSE OF PURPOSE IN RECENT DAYS IN "LEBANON"...

A WARNING TO ALL THOSE MUSLIM ACTIVISTS, THEIR FAMILIES, THEIR RELIGIOUS LEADERS IN THEIR MOSQUES AND BOOKSHOPS AND CHARITIES IN THE WEST!

WE ARE THE GOVERNMENTS HERE...
LOOK TO THOSE OF US IN THE UNITED STATES GOVERNMENT, THE SENATE AND THE CONGRESS...
LOOK TO THOSE OF US IN THE UNITED KINGDOMS GOVERNMENT...

LOOK TO YOUR SO CALLED FRIENDS WHO OFFERED YOU A RUN TO MAKE "PEACE"...

WE HAVE THE POWER AND THE FORCE TO TAKE CONTROL
THESE GOVERNMENTS FROM THE BORDERS OF RUSSIA TO THE RIVER NILE TO THE MOUNTAINS OF LEBANON TO THE DESERTS OF ARABIA...AS PROMISED TO THE "JEWISH PEOPLE" A "GREATER ISRAEL"

IT GROWS DAY BY DAY...WE GROW STRONGER DAILY MUSLIMS GROW WEAKER AND MORE DISUNITED...OUR "REVENGE" WILL BE VISITED ON YOUR COMMUNITIES SHORTLY...WE KNOW OUR ENEMIES...WE KNOW HOW TO DEAL WITH THEM...!

MAKE PEACE NOW...STOP YOUR DEMONSTRATION THE UNIVERSITY CAMPUSES...
STOP YOUR SPEAKERS NOW!
STOP OPPOSING US OR THE SAME AS HAS HAPPENED TO LEBANON WILL BE VISITED ON YOUR MOSQUES, YOUR FAMILIES, YOUR LEADERS...

LOOK AT THE POWER WE HAVE HERE!

NO MATTER WHAT HAPPENS TO YOU MUSLIMS

WE CONTROL THE ECONOMY AND POLITICS OF THESE STATES...
NO ONE DARES ATTACK US ANY MORE...
WHO DARED TO CRITICISE US FOR LEBANON...
WHERE IS THE U.N. OR THE USA OR THE UK...WITH US...PART OF US...
NO MORE "WEAK JEWS" TO SLAUGHTER...
WE NOW SLAUGHTER OUR ENEMIES AS PROMISED TO US BY THE "ALMIGHTY".

OUR ARM IS LONG AND IF OUR PEOPLE ARE ATTACKED OUTSIDE OF ISRAEL WE WILL RESPOND AGAINST THE "MUSLIM COMMUNITY" AROUND THE WORLD...OUR UNITS ARE ALREADY IN PLACE AND TRAINED...BE WARNED MUSLIMS YOUR LIVES ARE OURS LIKE THE SHEEP TO THE BUTCHER... YOU WILL BE DELIVERED INTO OUR HANDS AS HAS BEEN "WRITTEN" IN THE "TORAH" AND "TALMUD".
REMEMBER AS WE KNOW WHERE TO SEND THIS "WARNING" OUR UNITS KNOW WHERE TO COME EVEN TO YOUR "HOMES"...IF OUR FAMILIES ARE NOT SAFE THEN YOUR PARENTS, WIVES AND CHILDREN ARE LEGITIMATE TARGETS AS ARE YOUR HOMES, PLACES OF WORK, RESTAURANTS AND MOSQUES...WE WILL HAVE REVENGE!!!

THE "KHANE CHAI" AND ITS "FIGHTERS' WHO PROTECT THE JEWISH FAITH AND PEOPLE!

Hate mail 1996: faxed in thousands to prominent Muslims in the wake of the Israeli invasion of Lebanon

SAMI ZUBAIDA

Trajectories of political Islam

ISLAM has become a dominant idiom for the expression of a range of different political positions, social aspirations and frustrations. There is a logic to this idiom, but one that is not always followed through because of its involvement in political and social arenas of contestation.

The logic of the Islamist position is quite simple. A Muslim can only worship God and obey his commands in the company of other believers constituting a virtuous community. In practice, throughout Muslim history, this community was constituted by the immediate grouping of village, urban quarter, guild or Sufi brotherhood. Each was corporately organised under patriarchal, notable and/or religious authority, which demanded and enforced obedience to a code of social ethics. It was always assumed and accepted that outside the boundaries of this community (and boundaries were not always clearly defined) there were sundry others who could have been morally lax, of doubtful piety, or indeed non-Muslim. These were only combated or opposed when they were thought to impinge on the life of the community: we have examples from Syrian and Egyptian cities of complaints to the Qadi courts by neighbourhoods against particular houses, individuals, shops or cafes for moral infringements, sexual or to do with drink, drugs or entertainments. Repeated complaints and stern edicts made it clear that these activities continued to flourish. That is to say, the logic of virtue was authoritarian but limited in its scope to the immediate community whose boundaries were variable, and which left many islands of laxity between the corporate groups.

Modern Islamism, starting with the Muslim Brothers, founded in Egypt in 1928, is based on the assumption that the modern nation-state is the community of believers: that is to say, the ethical totalitarianism of the corporate community is now extended to the nation as a whole, assumed to be a Muslim nation. Hassan al-Banna, the founder of the Muslim Brotherhood in Egypt (d. 1949), argued in a book entitled *The Reform of Self and Society*, that the mission facing the Muslim is first to reform individual hearts and minds, and on the basis of that to reform society, and ultimately the good society will install the virtuous state. A more recent advocate proclaimed that historically Muslims could worship within their separate communities and ignore the state which was external to their lives. Under modern conditions of state intrusiveness into all aspects of social life this is no longer possible: for society to remain Muslim, the state must be Islamised.

It is interesting that this totalitarian logic of the Muslim nation was not followed by religious authorities and circles in Egypt and elsewhere until recent times. Secularists look back with nostalgia to the earlier decades of this century and until the 1970s, when cultural and artistic productions and entertainments were left well alone by religious authorities, who only reacted against direct challenges to what they regarded as their proper spheres of authority, to do with interpretations of religious sources. Otherwise, the modern spheres of art, culture, journalism and politics were not meddled with, assumed to be outside the reach and authority of religious institutions. It was mostly the modern trend exemplified in the Muslim Brotherhood which riled against what it considered to be the manifestations of corruption and decadence fostered and imposed by European power. This was, and remains, a kind of cultural nationalism, differentiated from its political counterparts by its exclusivist rejection of 'imported' culture.

The Muslim Brotherhood was from its foundation till the 1970s one oppositional political trend amongst many, the others being secular nationalist, liberal and socialist. It identified the left as its main enemy and rival, and the left branded it fascist, sharing with that ideology authoritarian corporatism and an organicist view of social unity, to be guarded against the divisiveness of political parties and class struggles. The fortunes of Islamism, including the Brotherhood, varied over the decades of the twentieth century with the ebbs and flows of political events. For the most part it was on the defensive against secular forces, and was specially eclipsed by Nasserism and other nationalist/'socialist' forces at the heyday of nationalism in the 1950s and 1960s. In Iran, Iraq and Sudan, powerful Communist Parties with mass organisations dominated the oppositional political field, with Islamists relegated to the margins. After the Arab defeat in the 1967 war with Israel, the Egyptians still rallied to Nasser when he offered his resignation, and the PLO founded in the aftermath was predominantly nationalist with strong leftist elements. Maoist and Guevarist insurrectionism became fashionable in oppositional politics of these days, in Iran, Turkey and the Arab world.

These leftist and liberationist ideologies played an important part in the ferment leading to the Iranian revolution of 1979. They enlivened both Islamic and secular political forces, notably in the advocacy of Ali Shari'ati (d.1977) who restated liberationist and Marxist themes in terms of Shia motifs, symbols and myths (at the cost of logic and coherence). These ideas reconciled the predominantly secular left and nationalist forces that made the revolution, to the Islamic leadership, organisation and finance. They were to be largely jettisoned by the mullah regime which followed, and which only kept the anti-imperialist rhetoric.

It is in this guise that the Iranian revolution attracted popular sentiment all over the region. The Iranian people, it seemed to many, had spoken, and their language is Islam. Where nationalism and the left failed, it seemed, Islam succeeded, because it spoke to the 'people'. The impact of these perceptions of the Iranian revolution in the region cannot be overestimated. It contributed to the decline in the credibility of the left and the various brands of secular nationalism. These were already in crisis because of their associations with governments and policies that appeared increasingly corrupt and incompetent, which did not deliver on any of their promises on development, participation or national power and dignity. Israel and America were more dominant than ever in the region, and the many years of Nasserism and Ba'athism, of military juntas and crippling military budgets, all seemed to have come to nothing. The reorientation towards the West and capitalism in Egypt and elsewhere, and finally the collapse of Communism and the Soviet Union exacerbated the crisis of the left and its credibility. Increasingly, political Islam came to be the dominant oppositional idiom.

Two major social and ideological sources of political Islam may be identified, the nationalist and the conservative. Many aspects of the ideologies and policies of political Islam can be seen as a development from secular nationalism and leftist motifs: anti-imperialism, anti-Israel, statist economic policies aimed at national strength and independence, in a framework of dependency theory and third-worldism, and the populist

Mubarak's Egypt: government propaganda film, The Terrorist, *denouncing Islamic terrorism*

rhetoric with an authoritarian frame of mind. These were the radical ideas behind the Iranian revolution, and which in other forms continue to animate the politics of intelligentsia elites in the Arab world and Turkey.

The conservative source is exemplified by Saudi Arabia. Its emphasis is on religious observance, repressive social ethics centred on the family and women, obedience to authority and a highly censorious stance to culture, art and intellectual products. Many Islamists, including Muslim Brothers in Egypt have close connections with Saudi Arabia, through work and business connections (Islamist businessmen tend to be in this category). Many religious and charitable activities in the region are financed by Saudi sources. Many cultural and media products in Egypt and elsewhere depend on the Saudi market, and are self-censoring. Many *ulama* and religious leaders have intimate Saudi connections and dependencies. These factors constitute a formidable influence on the political and cultural arenas. We must not forget also the enormous appeal of this brand of Islamic conservatism to many sectors of society reacting against what they see as the liberating and corrupting effects of modern social processes, and the quest by the rich, the influential and the notable to tighten social controls and ensure compliance with authority. We should note that this strand, broadly labelled *salafi* (following in the steps of the good ancestors), characterises both the respectable sector of *ulama*, dignitaries and bourgeoisie, and the violent Islamic groups: they differ in methods and styles, not ideas and objectives.

THE 'LOGIC' of the Islamist political position as outlined in the foregoing would seem to rule out democracy: it has a unitary and organicist vision of society. In more recent times, however, we hear many Islamist calls for democracy, some explicitly supporting political pluralism, electoral contest and alternation of governments as a result of these contests. These calls, however, would seem to contradict the practices of actually existing Islamic authorities. Hassan al-Tourabi, perhaps the most powerful man in Islamic Sudan, has over the years advocated democracy, which has led some Sudanese to distinguish between home-model Tourabi, and the export model! The unanimous emphasis on the application of the *sharia*, coupled with Islamist activities in Egypt against cultural and intellectual products, whether from the respectable Al-Azhar censorship committees or the intimidation from the violent groups (and these two do not differ ideologically) do not accord with the acceptance of pluralism. Do we conclude, with many of the secularists, that these calls are hypocritical, intended to gain acceptability and power, subsequently to be abandoned in favour of naked authoritarianism?

My answer is a qualified 'no'. I believe that there are a number of Islamic intellectuals in Egypt, Turkey and elsewhere who are genuinely seeking an accommodation, others who accept democracy as a pragmatic necessity to do with involvement in political contest and the struggle for constituencies of support, and yet others who call for democracy, but attach particular meanings to the word.

Let us first consider the latter category, including Tourabi. They consider democracy to be a direct correspondence between the people, conceived as a historical formation with Islam as its essential identity, and a state which expresses that identity. Secular states are despotic because they don't represent the people, and democracy is the rectification of this situation by establishing an Islamic state. The totalitarian implications of this view are clear. Tourabi, for instance, argues for direct democracy, established through popular referenda by electronic means on decisions facing the government. He finds this preferable to parties and institutions, which are divisive and corrupt. This view, then, is fully in accord with the totalitarian and organicist logic of Islamism.

A second attitude to democracy is exemplified in positions such as those of the leaderships of the Muslim Brotherhood in Egypt and the Refah Partisi (Welfare Party) in Turkey. These have a pragmatic attitude to democracy. Engaged in political and electoral contest, they have to balance their positions between appeal to moderate middle-class voters sympathetic to Islam but fearful of extreme measures, while at the same time satisfying their core constituencies of conservative Islamists demanding the *sharia*. Slogans and sound-bites involving democracy and pluralism, selectively used, can be useful for both ends. The more these groups are subject to political demands and the needs for compromise, the more they are likely to play the democratic game. By the same token, under conditions of social crisis and strife, they are even more likely to return to the authoritarian logic of their positions, especially if they share in state power.

A third attitude is that of political nationalist and reformist Islamists. In Egypt, this is now crystallising into a distinct trend, critical and increasingly separate from the conservative *salafis*. These are groups of intellectuals who see their political endeavour as a continuation of the national project started by Nasserism, and now carried on in populist Islamist terms. It is exemplified in Egypt by the group attempting to found a new political party, Hizb al-Wasat, the Middle Party. Why this tendency looks to democracy and pluralism is precisely because it wants to join forces with other national elements which are not Islamic. The founders of Hizb al-Wasat, for instance, include a number of Copts, and its leaders look to alliances with non-Islamic Nasserists. The Labour Party, an old established party now under Islamist hegemony, boasts the inclusion of Nasserists. Indeed, the declared quest of many of these intellectuals is for unity and consensus between national political and social forces outside the state for a programme of social and economic regeneration. Of course, Nasserists and other nationalists were not known for their democratic

Islamic Sudan: Hassan al-Tourabi, mover behind the Islamisation of Sudan

commitments. It would seem though that the contingencies of the present situation have driven them and their Islamic counterparts to the language of democracy and civil society.

The lively Turkish intellectual and political scene offers another example of these developments. One trend there is that associated with the notion of 'multiple law communities'. It argues that Islam is not about the state, but community, and that the quest for the Islamic state has distorted the central message of the faith, and that existing Islamic states are but mirror images of the modern, oppressive nation-state. The solution sought is a minimal state coexisting with multiple communities, each living by its own laws and norms, some religious, some not. This utopian quest has nevertheless inspired a pluralist outlook, as well as slogans for the more liberal Islamic politicians. There are signs that intellectuals of this tendency are now entering political alliance with some Islamic politicians, such as Racap Ergogan, the mayor of Istanbul, known for his reformist stance and opposition to the conservative hardliners of the Refah leadership.

What chance do these reformist forces stand against the bulwark of conservative Islam and its statist and authoritarian thrusts? The signs are not encouraging. The conservatives command resources and institutions, and many of them are in implicit or explicit collaboration with state interests, personnel and agencies.

THE IDEA of the 'secular' state under attack from Islamists is a myth, even in 'secular' Turkey. The Egyptian constitution enshrines the *sharia* as the main source of legislation. The Al-Azhar personnel and committees enjoy an increasing power of censorship. Saudi sensibilities ensure a large measure of cultural and media censorship. The government, while engaged in bloody suppression of the violent Islamic groups, is at the same time incorporating and endorsing many of their ideas and advocacies, coming from the more respectable dignitaries. The outcome of the Abu Zaid case was not the state refusing Islamist arguments on *hisbah*, but incorporating the authoritarian powers under that heading into the state. The state and its security agencies tacitly accept the provision of welfare services to the poor by Islamic groups, which maintains authoritative social control. It only combats these groups when they enter into explicit political opposition backed by violence. Informally, state personnel at all levels have ties of ideology and material interests with Islamic groups and institutions. There is a cosy relation between the Ministry of Social Affairs and the Islamic institutions and charities it oversees, to the benefit of its functionaries. The scandals that broke out in the mid-1980s about the Islamic investment companies showed the close connections they enjoyed to high functionaries, politicians, and leading *ulama*, to the mutual benefits of all. There is, then, a kind of symbiosis between Islamists and the state, in directions which reinforce the authoritarian thrust of both. Islamic intellectuals calling for democracy and pluralism are, like their secular counterparts, fearful of the spectre of these combinations. ❏

Sami Zubaida *is a reader in sociology at Birkbeck College, University of London*

DJAMAL ZITOUNI

War to the last

The first known policy statement from Algeria's Armed Islamic Groups offers no quarter to the enemies of Islam

ALGERIA is a 'land of war and Islam' where 'miscreants, people of the Book [Christians] and polytheists' must be killed in the name of *jihad*. This is the message delivered to the world in the first known attempt at political discourse by Djamal Zitouni, head of the GIA (Islamic Armed Groups) in Algeria. It presents Zitouni, *'emir'* — supreme leader — of the GIA, as the foremost radical theoretician of the armed Islamic struggle.

Other than that he is in his thirties and is the son of an Algiers chicken farmer, little is known of the inflammatory *emir* aka Abou Abderahmane Amine. It was he who he claimed responsibility for the kidnapping and execution of seven French monks in May, shocking even those close to him in the cohorts of the faithful.

A copy of the crudely produced 60-page *Rules for Salafis and the Duties of Mujaheddin,* was deivered to AFP (Agence France Presse) for wider dissemination via the western media. While most authorities agree on its authenticity, they detect the hand of Islamic experts in its finer points since Zitouni is thought to be relatively uneducated. It is written in classical Arabic and embellished throughout with verses from the Quran. Its author claims that the entire judicial council of the GIA welcomed its appearance; its purpose, he adds in the introduction is to 'ensure that the whole world knows about the GIA' particularly the *mujaheddin* — fighters for Islam.

It sets out the exceedingly tough rules and code of the movement, particularly those governing the allegiance of 'soldiers' to their *emir*. 'Anyone who leaves the GIA is a target for execution,' says Zitouni. There is a membership form at the end of the publication.

'*Jihad* must continue to the Day of Judgement,' announces Zitouni. 'Algeria is *Dar-ul-Islam* — the holy land of war and Islam — where people will be treated according to their faith or their apostasy; *jihad* against unbelievers, people of the Book and polytheists is the duty of every Muslim.' Miscreants include all current Muslim rulers — kings, princes, presidents and governments. As in Algeria, where the GIA has vowed to overthrow the state and its institutions, no 'dialogue, ceasefire nor reconciliation' with their likes is possible. All communities and cultures outside Islam, be they Communist, capitalist, nationalist, democratic, secular, as well as the Shia in Iran and Syria, are anathema.

The GIA claims to be the sole standard-bearer of *jihad* in Algeria. Other movements like FIS (Islamic Salvation Front) and its armed wing AIS (Islamic Army of Salvation) are apostates. Over the past few months, there has been a good deal of settling of scores between Algeria's rival armed groups. The precise number of confrontations and deaths is difficult to establish, but the battle lines seem to be drawn between two broad tendencies: the *salafi* — those who follow in the traditions of the good ancestors — who believe in a Muslim International and to which Zitouni's group of the GIA is attached, and the *Jez'ara* who propagate a national brand of Islam for Algeria.

Zitouni's tract includes a history of the GIA from the foundation of the first cell in August 1991 and of successive leaders. Zitouni himself took over the leadership from Cherif Gousmi after the latter had been killed by security forces in September 1994.

But the death of a leader is neither here nor there: '*Jihad* will continue to the final victory,' swears the unstoppable emir. 'All means justify the end, even if this means that unweaned babes, children and the poor must die. The preservation of religions is more important than a single human life.'

• *It is reported from Algeria that Zitouni's first venture into publishing could also be his death warrant. Shocked by his murder of the French monks, other groups under the GIA umbrella who see his form of radical extremism as a liability, have sworn to execute him.*

Translated from Libération, *Morocco by Judith Vidal-Hall*

JOHN SIMPSON

Afghan cockpit

The Taliban are the most extreme Islamist movement in the world. Their attempt to overthrow Kabul's Islamic government has reduced the country to rubble

'THE STRUGGLE of the people of Afghanistan against the Soviet invader is the struggle of free men and women the world over.'

There was a time when Ronald Reagan seemed to speak for many of us on this. Afghanistan was a beautiful, backward country which had been hit with all the force of the late twentieth century weaponry. Its crime was a desire to remain independent.

'Why,' asked Margaret Thatcher at a press conference in 1980, 'does the BBC insist on calling those brave mujaheddin 'rebels'? They are freedom-fighters, and that is what the BBC should call them.'

Times change. A few weeks ago, as I was waiting to cross the Pakistani border into Afghanistan, I read in the local press an account of another press conference by Lady Thatcher. She had just given it in Islamabad, the Pakistani capital, where she was promoting the latest volume of her memoirs. She had talked at length, according to the papers, about East-West relations and the end of the Cold War. She had talked about British policy towards Pakistan. But there was no mention of Afghanistan. She had come to a country which had been intimately associated with the war against the Russians, and where two million Afghan refugees still lived, and she managed to say nothing whatever about the subject which had once exercised her so strongly.

Afghans of all persuasions find it hard to understand why their country has been forgotten. To us, perhaps, it is easy: once it was a piece on the international chess board, and now the game has changed. End of story. They, however, believed all the geopolitical rhetoric about being at the crossroads of Asia, and the praise that was heaped on them by their western friends. Asia, however, has found other crossroads, and the world has found other crises to worry about. What happens in Afghanistan is no longer relevant.

Yet by any standards it is terrible. When my colleagues and I were in Kabul I walked down a mile-long stretch of road leading to the outskirts of town. Once there were two universities along this road and five schools. Now there is nothing but ruins and rubble. Sarajevo, by comparison with this, got off lightly. The mud brick, yellow-grey in colour, has been smashed into piles of little more than dust. An occasional page from a textbook fluttered among the ruins. Everything else worth having had long since been looted, regardless of the danger from anti-personnel mines and exploded shells.

None of this was done by the Russians. On the contrary, it had been with Russian help that the universities and schools were built up. This was the result of the fighting between the mujaheddin groups since the Russian withdrawal. With the help and encouragement from Afghanistan's neighbours, who have no particular interest in seeing so turbulent a country at peace, faction after faction has taken on the relatively moderate groups which form the government of Kabul. Gulbuddin Hekmatyar has sometimes fought his way into the government coalition as prime minister, and sometimes been ejected forcibly from it. His Hezb-i-Islami group had strong support from Pakistan, which fought out its proxy battles with India and Russia, backers of the Kabul government, on the territory of Afghanistan. General Dustam, with covert help from Russia, fought the government troops along this road and was responsible for the worst of the destruction. The Shi'ite groups, backed by Iran, flared up in occasional rebellion.

'This is what they do best — fight each other,' said a superb government figure in one of Afghanistan's neighbours. With your help, I said as politely as I could, and he shook his head in mock rebuke. For people like him, Afghanistan is not a place to be taken seriously. It doesn't matter; it is a political black hole, without effective government, from which nothing emerges but heroin and casualties too bad for the local hospitals to cope with.

Nowadays, again with Pakistani help, another group is challenging the Kabul government. The Taliban — the word means 'religious students' — began in the refugee camps around the Pakistani border town of Quetta and swept across into Afghanistan in 1994, enraged at the failure of the government to impose the basics of fundamentalist Islam. They are not particularly good fighters, but they are Pashtu-speakers who have played intelligently on the linguistic divisions inside Afghanistan and have gained the support of many groups which disliked the lordly ways of the predominantly Tajik-speaking government in Kabul. Many of the Taliban's greatest gains have been achieved through making deals, rather than on the field of battle. Now they control half the territory and almost half the population of Afghanistan, from Herat in the west to the border with Pakistan, and their forces are besieging the capital, Kabul, itself. The Taliban's main centres, Qandahar and Herat, are now on the Pakistani telephone system, and Pakistani banks flourish in several of their towns and cities.

The Taliban are probably the most extreme Islamic fundamentalist group in the world. By comparison, Iran and even Saudi Arabia seem positively liberal. Their main base, Qandahar, is strangely empty of women, and those few who appear on the streets are covered from head to foot in the traditional *burkhas*, with a panel of lace to hide their features. On either side of the road that leads into the centre of the city stand two rickety steel towers. The Taliban have strung up old televisions and video-cassettes on them, hanging them with recording tape like the bodies of executed criminals from gibbets. The message is clear: television is evil, because it presumes to capture the likeness of living creatures and turn them into graven images.

Qandahar is not, therefore, the easiest place for a television team to work. An aggressive young mullah was appointed to chaperone us, and he had instructions not even to let us film the hanging television sets. We did anyway, since he had little idea of the scope a cameraman has for filming surreptitiously; but we found it impossible to persuade any senior figure in the Taliban to record an interview with us on camera. Some, more moderate, were sympathetic to the idea, but felt their position within the organisation would suffer if it were known that we had made a graven image of them.

On our last day we went to see the Taliban minister of health, Mullah Balouch. He had a fearsome reputation: a strong supporter of the punishments defined in the *sharia*, or Islamic law, he tried to persuade the surgeons under his control to cut off the hands and feet of convicted criminals. If they refused, he did it himself. By all accounts he rather enjoyed it.

Afghanistan 1995: students of violence and repression

We found him in his office, surrounded by a couple of dozen petitioners. When he saw us he waved them away. With the camera running, I went over to him and asked him if he would consider giving us an interview. It never occurred to me that he might. Yet Mullah Balouch turned out to be a liberal — in everything except the *sharia* punishments, that is.

'It is idolatry to show a person's face, since a graven image can be made from that. But if you show me down to the waist, no graven image can be made of that.'

'Absolutely,' I said, not understanding a word of it; and we showed him down to the waist.

He proved to be a frank interviewee, except on the question of his own involvement with the punishments. He absolutely denied cutting off anyone's hands or feet himself, even though it was a matter of public knowledge. Perhaps he realised the effect it might have on a western audience if he admitted it. But he insisted that there was nothing strange in a minister of health's persuading hospital surgeons to do it. I didn't disagree with him. Liberals were in short supply in the Taliban without falling out with one.

Unless the Taliban do a deal with some mujaheddin group inside Kabul, they are unlikely to capture the city and win the war. Maybe their Pakistani friends and backers keep Afghanistan too busy with its own civil strife for it to be able to have an effect on its neighbours.

The real price for all the fighting is paid by the ordinary people of the city. The Taliban say they do not deliberately target civilians, unlike Hezb-i-Islami and General Dustam's forces. That appears to be true; yet the rockets the Taliban use are so inaccurate that they kill and maim people virtually every day. The hospitals are full of terribly wounded people, who have no-one to look after them and no cause for hope.

One senior figure in the Kabul government maintains that a single week's shuttle diplomacy by the Americans, the British or the French could bring this latest phase of fighting in Afghanistan to an end. Perhaps; but the chances that President Clinton or John Major might somehow want to get involved in the situation when elections are near are impossibly remote. The Afghans themselves, with the help of their neighbours, have ensured that the country is seen merely as a cockpit for different factions to fight in.

Afghanistan served its purpose in the 1980s, as far as the West is concerned; it helped to bring down Communism in the Soviet Union and eastern Europe. Now it doesn't matter. It can be abandoned to cynical warlords, to the agents of outside powers, to ultra-extremists who hang television sets and use surgeons and hospital equipment as part of their judicial system. It's a couple of pages in the memoirs: nothing more. ❑

John Simpson is *BBC foreign affairs editor*

Two letters to one President

On 18 May, the Tehran daily, *Akhbar*, published two letters side by side on its front pages. The first, from the Muslim intellectual Abdolkarim Sorush, complained of threats to his life and teaching from the Ansar-e Hezbollah (Supporters of the Party of God). The second was the latter's reply attacking Iran's 'secular visionary, Mr Deliverance'

Tehran University, 1994: Sorush and students

How long, Mr President, how long?

To the honourable President of the Islamic Republic of Iran, His Eminence Hojjat ol-Eslam val-Moslemin Akbar Hashemi-Rafsanjani, Greetings and regards,

I would hereby like to convey to you the following information, which uniquely concerns the realm of education and human rights, in order to seek Your Eminence's guidance and advice.

Your Eminence is no doubt aware of the heinous attacks and abuse I have been subjected to during the last year from certain pressure groups and the newspapers associated with them. The Intelligence Ministry, too, has played its part — by summoning me repeatedly, threatening me and imposing limitations on me — in tightening the noose, depriving me of my human rights and making it easier for my opponents to do and say whatever they like. My deliberate stance throughout all this has been to be patient and silent. Their terror and threats have reached such a point that no-one dares offer me teaching posts any more. In other words, they have also closed this door to me. Only one course has been allocated to me at Tehran University. Even so, nowadays, when I arrive at the college of social sciences to teach my course in 'the philosophy of social sciences' at the official invitation of Tehran University, I am confronted with a range of impediments and serious verbal and physical intimidation. On each occasion, a group of people (and everyone knows exactly who they are, where they come from and what their intentions are) gather outside the college, on motorcycles and on foot, and make every effort to bring about confrontations and even bloodshed (talk of bloodshed came from one of the invaders when he was speaking to the deputy head of the college). At times, I have no option but to enter the college secretly and furtively, and to try to teach my course faced with distressed and frightened students, leaving my lecture half finished and beating a hasty retreat. At other times, I do not even manage to do this much and my students are left high and dry with no lecturer and no lecture. The honourable head of Tehran University and the head of the college of social sciences have done their utmost to quell the disturbances, but their efforts have remained unsuccessful because of overt and covert support for the invaders from a number of overt and covert institutions (including the representative office of the supreme jurisconsult [the office of Khamenei's representative at the university]; and, in fact, the troublemakers are constantly growing in number and in their range of paraphernalia. On one particular occasion a threatening letter, signed by the Hezbollah, was handed to me in the middle of a lecture which spoke of 'putting their all' into getting rid of me and expelling me from the class; talk, in other words, of violence and bloodshed once again. (The letter is still in my possession.)

The latest incident has to do with an invitation to me from the Islamic Association of Amir Kabir College to take part in a seminar commemorating the martyrdom of Professor Motahhari. Even before this invitation was publicised, the Intelligence Ministry harassed and frightened my family with repeated telephone calls. Resorting to pressure and intimidation, it bans and forbids me from taking part in the lecture, doing its utmost to deprive this humble servant of his indisputable right, without so much as a by-your-leave and without any rhyme or reason. Instead of bringing the pressure groups to order and ensuring the safety of knowledge-lovers, it goes down the crooked road of forcing lecturers to be silent and to break their promises in order to guarantee the security of the violators of security. The troublemakers, for their part, also came on to the stage even before the event, turning the college into their own parade-ground with rallies and demonstrations. And they are again (according to the head of Amir Kabir College) speaking of bloodshed at the college on the day of the lecture.

Mr President: My simple and straightforward question — as someone who is not in the least the lawbreaking, unruly or troublemaking type — to you — as someone who has repeatedly spoken of the dignity, security and liberty of scholars — is this: how long must the academics of this land pay the penalty for the disruptive and lawless behaviour of twisted and irresponsible groups; how long must they be silent, huddled in corners, pretending to be deaf and dumb, suffering insults and threats, enduring the violation of their own and their families' dignity and security, and witnessing with their own eyes the fact that the law-breakers are safe and the law-abiding tormented? Had the perpetrators of the ugly disturbances that took place at Tehran University's technical college on 11

October 1995 been properly dealt with and punished — instead of being praised and lauded — would they still be creating trouble as they are today? Have you been informed of the scandalous behaviour, perpetrated before the frightened and disbelieving eyes of university students, by the gang of people, mounted and on foot, who gather at the college of social sciences each week — with the security forces doing nothing to stop them and even encouraging them? Has the education minister told you about these incidents? Are these ugly events in keeping with the dignity of a distinguished institute of learning? Are these despicable deeds, which have no sense or purport other than to undermine the job security and freedom of action of lecturers and researchers and to insult the university blatantly, a source of pride and honour for the universities of this country? Do you, as the chairman of the Cultural Revolution Council, endorse them? And have you taken any steps to put an end to them?

How long must the academics of this land pay the penalty for the disruptive and lawless behaviour of twisted and irresponsible groups: how long remain silent, pretend to be deaf and dumb?

Mr President: During the past eight months, I have, for the good of the country, patiently and agonisingly refused all lecture invitations and I have not spoken at any public gatherings. I have even disregarded and left unanswered the flood of insults and accusations that have been hurled at me from the country's Friday prayer pulpits and newspapers. In other words, I have foregone my undeniable rights. I can see, however, that not only have I not gained anything as a result of this but, with the offenders becoming increasingly more brazen, my job security and my very life are now in danger. In addition to receiving open and secret intimidating letters, I am today threatened by law-breakers, all of whose names and details are known to the country's officials — yet nothing whatsoever is done to break the blades of their insolence.

Mr President: Thanks be to God, I have never cried out against these wounds. I have continued to smile, albeit with a leaden heart. I have not been broken by the jeers of the jealous or allowed myself to be drawn into dissension and discord. I have sought refuge in the narrowest alleyways of comfort. I have walked away from the taunts of the petty tyrants and, in the spirit of Abraham, I have tried to see flowers amid the flames. But I would like to ask you: has this country come to such a pass that, to get to their classes, teachers must say their final prayers, risk life and limb, and walk into the jaws of danger? Does this state, too, need Galileos or Giordano Brunos?

M r President: How can I speak to my students about hope in the future, about the freedom and courage to think, about the open and welcoming climate of society when I can see for myself that each of these ideas has now been transformed into an unpardonable sin for which I myself am constantly punished by pressure groups and associations totally lacking in culture? How can I say to my students that, in this land, they do not ram the ships of lovers of learning, that they do not repay the efforts of someone — who has, without any demands or expectations, devoted a full 30 of his 50 years to research and study in the fields of epistemology and religion, seeking to unravel philosophical problems, writing, translating, teaching, serving the education of his students with unswerving dedication — with persecution, blows, daggers and insults? And how, most heart-breaking of all, can one bear to see that all this evil and treachery, all these inquisitions and impositions, are perpetrated in the beloved name of religion, the *sharia* and the *velayat* [religious guardian ie. Khamenei]?

M r President: The rabble-rousers and troublemakers have now pushed their confrontation with this country's thinkers to the point of enmity against the country itself. In their attempts at character assassination and the disparagement of individuals, they have, without realising it, turned their attacks against the culture, traditions, history and virtues of this innocent land. Acting on the basis of spite and prejudice, they are distorting and besmirching the good name and honour of our country in the eyes of foreigners and future generations. They are founding an evil and wicked tradition that is entirely out of keeping with the ancient cultural customs and the benevolent religious practices of this country. I am turning to you with my grievance now not just for my own sake, but because of the injustice that is being perpetrated against the honour and goodness of our exemplary culture; because of the harm that is being done to the cultural acumen of our people; because of the unholy and concerted efforts that are being made to distort the truth and to glorify violence; because of the crooked foundations that are being laid in the relationship between individuals and learning; and because of the insults and humiliations that are being inflicted on education and on universities. I am bringing my plaint to you and I emphatically expect you, in view of your legal powers and cultural and religious responsibilities, not to turn away indifferently from this cultural infection but to strive, like a doctor and a surgeon, to treat it and cure it. You can be certain that all the culture-lovers, well-wishers and justice-seekers of this land will support you and assist you, and they will applaud your good work in their hearts and with their deeds.

Mr President: I am sitting here mourning the loss of a university at which a group of people is now triumphantly celebrating the death of learning and the birth of barbarity; I sit here fearing for the sanctity and greatness of an institution that is being draped in scorn and ridicule; I fear for the grieving lecturers and students who look on in silence, with hopelessness and despair; I am thinking of the thousands upon thousands of hopes that have been torn away by this storm of wickedness and are drifting to the ground like dead autumn leaves; my heart goes out to the students whose rights have been so mindlessly and ruthlessly trampled underfoot and crushed. This is not just my story; it is the story of the hope, education and future of this country.

Mr President, the triumph of evil-doers would mean the defeat of our culture, the destruction of our hopes and the annihilation of our ideas. Do not let them snatch away these precious pearls. It is not seemly to look on in silence. Do not let them win.

What cloud is this now, casting its shadow
Over the entire world, not just over me?
Look up a moment, see what is being lost here:
Thousands of hopes, hopes that belong to all humanity.

With further regards,
Abdolkarim Sorush
9 May 1996

Translated by Nilou Mobasser

Mr Deliverance, we warn you

To the honourable President His Eminence Hojjat ol-Eslam val-Moslemin Akbar Hashemi-Rafsanjani, with greetings,

Your Eminence will no doubt be acquainted with us, although not by name. Contemporary history, too, is well acquainted with every single one of our slaughtered and blood-drenched brothers 'by fame'...

You know very well that we have no personal problems with any person or persons. Our hearts have no room left for personal sorrows or vendettas. How can our brothers, who have never felt any common cause with vengeance-seekers and who have practised the art of 'fighting without personal enmity' for years, now succumb to vendettas?! The people, who are accusing us of violence, themselves possess the most violent tongues and the most impudent pens, and their eyes are as bloodshot as their hearts are black...

In the course of a two-page letter, our secularist visionary! has uttered more than 10 lies and 100 insults, and he has, more than a dozen times, expressed anxiety that *Ansar* students wish to kill him. But he does not deign to explain even once why he refuses to give straight answers to their questions?! Nor does he say why they should have any wish to turn into a martyr or a hero such a contemptible person who is not even prepared to state his views openly and frankly?! It would be far better for the likes of him to die of jaundice and be exposed on their deathbeds...

Your Eminence, Mr President: We have never said that he and his like should not express their views. In recent years, the party of the secularists has had, and continues to have, access to the greatest number of written and spoken platforms in this country. Public funds are put at their disposal in greater quantities than anyone else and dozens of publications and university posts are under the control of the intellectual lackeys of the West. As God is our witness, the resources available in this country to Ansar students is about one-thousandth of those available to the secularist party. They have said everything they wanted to say in recent years and will continue to do so.

In the meantime, what we have been saying and will continue to say is nothing other than this:

1) In accordance with the clearly expressed will, directed at university students, of His Eminence the Imam [the late Khomeini], may God be satisfied with his deeds, the likes of 'Mr Deliverance' must not be allowed to propagate secularism, liberal morality and interests, and American ideology at the universities of the revolution using public resources; nor must they be permitted to recruit cadres for their party.

2) It would be far better if Mr Deliverance and the secularists, who are the mouthpieces of the West in Islamic Iran, stayed within their party headquarters and stated their political and ideological principles clearly and explicitly.

3) He must take part in a debate with Ansar students and answer our questions. The debate between the students and Sorush can take place over 15 sessions, under specific headings which will be announced by us. We students will ensure that there is full security at these sessions. Specific questions will be raised at the sessions based on his own statements, so that we may obtain crystal-clear responses in the presence of large or smaller audiences...

Ansar-e Hezbollah students
15 May 1996

Translated by Nilou Mobasser

ABDOLKARIM SORUSH

The functions and benefits of religion

Religion and state must be separated for neither will prosper while mullahs govern. Excerpts from a lecture first printed in *Kiyan*, 'a monthly journal in the field of philosophy and religion', November 1995

The cover of the Kiyan issue in which Sorush's lecture appeared lists articles by Mohammed Arkhoun (Algerian philosopher), Sheikh Fadlallah Nuri (Iranian cleric hanged by Reza Shah), Karl Popper on 'Knowing and not knowing', Jorge Casteneda on 'Intellectuals and government in Latin America' and Jeremy Hawthorne on 'Realism, modernism and post-modernism in the novel'

AN IMPORTANT QUESTION is raised at this point: What does religion have to say about the material world? Does religion also serve a function in ensuring our material welfare? I consider it my duty to state my own opinion quite frankly. The point I am going to make is not confined to Islam. It applies to all religions in general. In my opinion, religious teachings are aimed principally at the other world. In other words, they have to do with our well-being and welfare in the afterlife. And this is exactly what our principal expectation from religion is. This is precisely the need that drives us towards religion. This is our most essential lack as human beings who have eternal lives. It is, therefore, in this respect that we look to religion for guidance and assistance. To put it another way, if we did not have eternal lives and if there were no afterlife awaiting us, we would have no need for religion and the prophets of God would not approach us. The secret behind our need for religion is the eternal nature of our lives and the existence of an afterlife. The material world is the preface to and the hinterland of the afterlife. It is its quality as a prelude that has made the material world so dear to religion... In the words of Mowlana [Jalaluddin Rumi (1207-1273 CE) poet and mystic]:

Seek religion and, then, you will see
Favours and blessings and wealth aplenty
The other world is like a train of camels
This world, like heaps of wool
Pick wool and you'll be left without a camel
Pick a camel and you'll ne'er be without wool

I would, therefore, like to make a few brief points about this. First, when I say religion is principally aimed at the other world, this does not mean that it is of no use to this world. 'Being of use to this world' or 'bearing upon this world' is one thing; saying that 'in the beginning religion did not come into existence for this world or for material concerns' is another. We are not saying that religion is of no use to this world; what we are saying is that God did not, initially and essentially, send religion down to us for the sake of material things or to improve our wretched lives in this world. If religion had to do with material affairs, then it would have been sent to us even if there had been no afterlife. However, religion's overwhelming emphasis on the afterlife rules out this possibility. The reasonable thing to say is that this world must be administered on the basis of the intellect and rational management, and this has, in fact, been the case so far.

I had written somewhere that religious jurisprudence does not yield plans and programmes, and that 'planning in accordance with religious jurisprudence' is a patent absurdity. Some people did not take to this and felt it was unacceptable. Let us now see where the truth lies.

The most obvious and likely aspect or dimension of religion that touches upon life and welfare in this world is, precisely, 'religious jurisprudence'. Religious jurisprudence is a science derivative of rulings, and it is clear that it leads to commands, must dos and must not dos regarding social and individual life. Everyone who is of the opinion that religion lays out a programme for our lives in this world bases their claims on precisely such rulings of religious jurisprudence as pertaining to economics and politics. But this view can be disputed; I am emphasising and dwelling on religious jurisprudence here, because few people have made such claims about ethics or beliefs, and most of the people making these claims base their assertions on the rulings of religious jurisprudence.

Second, religious jurisprudence is an aggregate of rulings and 'ruling' is different from 'programme'; and, in order to manage our livelihoods we need something more than rulings. That is to say, we need, precisely, plans and programmes. Religious jurisprudence does not suffice for the organisation and running of material life. This is the essence of my reasoning and the sum total of what I am saying.

I do not think that anyone familiar with the nature of law and religious jurisprudence will need to think very long before confirming what is being said here. Religious jurisprudence is a religious version of a legal code; in exactly the same way that, outside the religious sphere and in non-religious societies, too, there are legal systems for dealing with material questions and for settling disputes. In religious societies and within the framework of the religious system in our country, we have religious jurisprudence instead of human and secular legal codes — and it plays exactly the same role. Both law and religious jurisprudence are there to solve legal problems.

Let us now ask if all the problems experienced in society and in life are legal problems? Are we free from all problems except legal ones? If we believe that all the problems in society are uniquely legal problems, then, of course, religious jurisprudence will contain solutions to all problems. That is, religious laws will hold the key to every aspect of believers' lives.

It is, however, axiomatic that only a small part of the problems experienced in life are legal problems; and these are problems that, in the main, take the form of disputes. As Ghazali [Abu Hamid Al-Ghazali (1058-1111 CE) philosopher, jurist and mystic] put it...in the first volume of his four-volume work *Revival of Sciences*: 'If people behave with justice in this world, conflicts will cease and religious jurisconsults will go out of business.' The meaning of the jurisconsults 'going out of business' is that they have achieved their desired end. It does not mean that they went out of business because their work was worthless. This is exactly like saying, if people looked after their health, doctors would go out of business... This should be a cause for joy among doctors, not a source for regret that there are no more patients. The ultimate aim of a doctor's work is healthy people and the attainment of this aim reveals the excellence of the doctor's work. What Ghazali is saying about religious jurisprudence (and, specifically, about its section on transactions) is very similar in nature...

Nonetheless, as we said, the problems of society are not confined to legal problems. For example, take the fact that the world's forest cover is in the process of destruction. Is this an entirely legal/jurisprudential problem?... Must we not try to seek a scientific solution to prevent the destruction?

Examples of this kind are endless and unlimited in number. Imagine that the country needs blood, that this blood must be free from germs and viruses, that it must be kept in special sanitised conditions, that there must be enough of it and so on. Are these legal matters? Even assuming that they have a legal dimension, can they be reduced to this? It is a source of wonder that there are people who believe that laws and religious jurisprudence can solve all of society's problems. This can only hold if all problems are legal and jurisprudential, and this is, in the end, untrue. Thus, when we say, religious jurisprudence does not provide us with plans and programmes, this is what we mean. We mean that it gives rulings but it does not produce programmes. Programming is the task of science, not the task of religious jurisprudence. It demands a scientific method. This is not to diminish religious jurisprudence, it is to recognise its limits and powers. The problems and difficulties of society are mainly scientific in nature, not jurisprudential. That is to say, resolving them is not the responsibility of religious jurisprudence, but of science. The question of how blood must be stored, the question of how agriculture should be run, how the forest cover can be preserved, how air pollution can be controlled and... [ellipsis in original] are all non-legal, scientific problems. Let me ask you now, do we need to solve these problems or not?

Turn to economics: are all economic problems legal problems? Legal problems rear their head when you usurp someone's land or when you act contrary to the regulations in a transaction. These are legal/jurisprudential problems; but the question of how inflation can be tackled is not. This is a scientific problem. There is really no need for any further examples. Most of society's problems are non-legal and non-jurisprudential and we must, therefore, turn to the non-legal and non-jurisprudential for their solutions. That 'non-legal and non-jurisprudential' thing consists of the sciences, which are products of human intellect and experience. Economics is a science. If anyone believes that the science of economics is the same as the science of economic rights, they are clearly mistaken. It is exactly the same if you take political science. It is not identical with the science of political rights. The science of health and medicine clearly differs from legal questions about health and medicine... It is most interesting to note that, today, in our country, a number of doctors hold a conference on medical jurisprudence — without any concern for medical ethics — and they believe that, if they solve all the problems regarding religious jurisprudence, they will have solved all ethical problems as well; as if religious jurisprudence could solve ethical problems. This is another error.

Look at management. Is management within the scope of religious jurisprudence? Management is a skill. Of course, it may happen that a manager or a worker commits an offence, at which time the regulations must be invoked. But what does the issue of whether a manager can successfully and honestly run an organisation or not have to do with the law or religious jurisprudence? Management is a skill based on psychology and sociology. The rules that are devised and put into effect for the optimum running of affairs are also based on psychological and sociological understandings. You can see, too, that a manager who acts strictly according to the rules is not necessarily a good manager. Imagine that 99 per cent of a workforce have committed an offence and that they are all punished according to the regulations. This would make for a rule-abiding organisation, but not a successful one. In other words, the observance of the law or religious jurisprudence does not necessarily guarantee that a society or an organisation is successful. Take a society, for example, in which 99 per cent of the marriages end up in divorce and in which everyone divorces their partner strictly in accordance with the dictates of religious jurisprudence. Such a society would be jurisprudentially correct, but it would not be a healthy society.

It is exactly the same when it comes to education, teaching or training; or industry, the construction of dams, road building, airport building, laying telephone lines, urban planning, running a municipality or... [ellipsis in original]. None of these is a legal/jurisprudential matter and no jurisconsult has drawn up or will draw up plans and programmes for them. They have not been discussed in any text on religious jurisprudence; no-one would even make such a claim. The essence of what I am saying, in other words, is that religious jurisprudence ensures the resolution of the jurisprudential problems of society, but not all of society's problems are jurisprudential and a society in strict adherence to religious jurisprudence is not necessarily a healthy society. We need something more than religious jurisprudence. Thus, the incorrect conception that religion and religious jurisprudence are all-encompassing must be amended. This conception is beneficial neither to religion nor to religious jurisprudence. One must not imagine that the all-embracing nature of religion means that religion has raised and solved every problem. Religion is complete, it is not comprehensive and there is a difference between completeness and comprehensiveness.

A clergyman has written that religious jurisprudence suffices for both rulings and for planning. Its sufficiency in terms of rulings can be accepted: 'For every event that occurs there is a divine ruling.' A ruling, however, is different from a plan. 'Plan' means an agricultural plan, an economic or a medical plan. None of these has anything to do with law or religious jurisprudence. And if anyone who has the slightest familiarity with religious jurisprudence, pauses to think carefully about it for a moment, they will easily agree with what is being said here.

We have thus examined the status of religious jurisprudence — the aspect of religion most related to the material world. Everyone who claims that religion is meant to see to the affairs of this world relies on exactly this aspect. ❏

Dr Abdolkarim Sorush was born in 1945 and educated in Iran and England. He is currently a research fellow at the Institute for Research in Humanities, and a lecturer in philosophy at Tehran University. He is author of some 20 books and a number of articles

Translated by Nilou Mobasser

PHOTO-FEATURE

Rangoon 1996: Aun San Suu Kyi addressing followers

Faces in a crowd

On 8 June, Aung San Suu Kyi addressed supporters of the National League for Democracy from her home for the first time since the SLORC government banned public gatherings there

'We always talk about the rule of law and try to persuade the authorities to do what is necessary to bring about the rule of law. We always speak about how important the law is in a country and in society. We repeatedly say that the law must be equal for all.

'We gather here because we all want democracy. When we say we want democracy, we are not referring simply to a goal we want to reach. It is in fact a means through which we can bring about

prosperity for our country.

To further the peace and prosperity of the country is the responsibility of the people in this country. The citizens of this country must first of all know their responsibilities and then carry them out dutifully. Only such citizens can build a democratic country.

'There are people both in Burma and abroad who doubt whether the Burmese are fit for democracy. But we believe the people have the ability.

I want you to understand how heavy the people's responsibility is. Don't be discouraged by this responsibility. Don't be discouraged that some people who want to take up that responsibility don't get the chance. Whenever you get the chance, take it up as a privilege. I want people to understand that, the greater the people's responsibility, the greater it is a test of the people's ability.

Our fundamental goal was to make headway toward achieving

(Above)The face of Burma 1996: child labourer caught on undercover camera
(Right, top) Faces in a crowd: listening to Aung San Suu Kyi
(Right, bottom) Mandalay 1996: welcome to our country

THE BIGGEST BOOK OF THE WORLD

TO ALL FOREIGN
VISITORS
WITH EFFECT FROM
1st SEPTEMBER 1994
ENTRANCE FEES WILL
BE CHARGED BY THE
TRUSTEES OF THE
MAHA LOKA MARAJIN
KUTHODAW PAGODA FOR
ADMISSION AT US$2
OR K-250 FOR EACH
VISITOR.

BOARD OF TRUSTEES

VISIT
MYANMAR YEAR
1996

democracy. That is why in our campaigning we worked to explain what democracy is. We pointed out what democratic methods are, and we looked to see to what extent that the people understood democracy. For we believed we could only achieve democracy to the extent the people understood it.

'We must not see our people as anonymous or as a faceless crowd. When we gather here, while Ba Ba U Kyi Mung and Ba Ba U Tin Oo speak, I try my best to remember the faces in the crowd. I don't want to acknowledge you simply as part of a crowd but want to recognise and value you as your very individual selves. I want to acknowledge that each and every one of you who has gathered here is an individual human being and important in your own right.

Ready for 1996?: new tourist hotel in Rangoon

Land of fear: forced labour prepares the country for tourists

I want to see each one of you as our co-workers and our supporters. Never doubt that we realise you are supporting our movement. Even if we don't get to know each one of you individually, I want you to know that we feel the power of your love every day.

'The next point concerns the construction of bridges, roads, and pagodas. We can't deny that building these is good. We never said it wasn't, but we did indicate that the authorities should consider how these construction projects are carried out.

'We have no reason to reject the open market system. We also indicated we would encourage tourism in a way that would benefit the country and that we would invite foreign investment.' ❏

Excerpts from speech of 8 June, courtesy Burma Action Group, London

HUMAN RIGHTS

CAROLINE MOOREHEAD

Post-war amnesia

When the Allies went to war for Gulf oil in 1991, they cloaked their intervention in the language of human rights. Today, they and the region have forgotten how to speak the words

IN 1991, the US-led international military forces went into Iraqi-occupied Kuwait loudly promising to bring human rights to the Arab world. Saddam Hussein and Iraq were to be a taught a lesson no-one could forget. Five years later, it is possible to see how far that promise proved illusory. At Sharm al-Shaykh in Egypt in March, when leaders from 29 countries met to discuss the suicide bombings in Israel by armed Islamist groups, the talk was all of terrorism and the enemy had become not Iraq but Iran. As Shimon Peres put it, 'the capital of terror' was Tehran, not Baghdad. With the new Likud government dragging the Israeli-Palestinian peace process into ruins; the spectre of Islamic fundamentalism effectively serving to legitimise the worst abuses from Bahrain and Saudi Arabia to Lebanon and Israel; and the principles of 'universality' and 'specificity' in tatters as cultural arguments dictate economic deals, the prospect for human rights in the Middle East has never looked more bleak.

It was not supposed to be like this. When the Iraqis invaded Kuwait in August 1990 the atrocities they committed soon confirmed — as Amnesty International and others had long reported but the West had chosen to ignore — that Iraq was a brutal and murderous nation. People now remembered that Saddam Hussein and his followers had gassed and exterminated many thousands of Kurds, that torture was routine in Iraqi prisons and summary executions had become the accepted method of disposing of dissidents. All this was now repeated in Kuwait and became a

Kuwait 1991: surrender of Iraqi troops

valid pretext for war. The timing of the invasion, too, was crucial. The Cold War was over, old alliances and allegiances were shifting, and there was a real feeling, in more parts of the world than had been possible for many years, that human rights were something not just desirable, but actually achievable if enough effort and goodwill went into them.

The 43-day-war was an excellent exercise in public relations. It was, as the US secretary of defence, Richard Cheney, put it, 'the most successful air-campaign in the history of the world'. In some ways, he was right. A vast collection of airplanes did rapidly establish superiority over the Iraqi forces. It was not, however, quite as clean and good as the publicity suggested. Several thousand civilians died in the bombing raids, Bedouin tents and civilian tankers were bombed, only nine per cent of weapons actually belonged to the much vaunted 'smart' variety, which could be suited to their targets, and the smashing of the electrical system reduced the Iraqi population to a 'pre-industrial age' with terrible effects on hospitals and water supplies — methods of war for the most part in breach of the First Additional Protocol of 1977 to the 1949 Geneva Convention. What was more, the Allies left behind them two — some say five — million unexploded 'bomblets' from cluster bombs which now lie, like landmines, waiting to explode when disturbed. In the first two years after the war, 1,600 civilians were killed by the bomblets, concealed in soft sand or shallow water; over 2,500 others were maimed.

These things were quickly forgotten. What has not proved so easy to ignore, as the new alliances created by the fighting have settled to some kind of pattern, have been the widespread human rights violations that followed swiftly on the war. No country in the region has remained untouched by them. When the Iraqi forces withdrew from Kuwait at the end of February 1991, martial law was declared by the Emir. Under cover of restoring order, 1,000 people were arrested, suspected collaborators were seized, tortured and killed; tens of thousands of Kuwait's Bedoon, longtime inhabitants denied Kuwaiti citizenship and who had fled the Iraqi invasion, were barred from returning home; others were deported in a sudden increase in repression. Palestinians, Jordanians, Sudanese and Yemeni were among those who 'disappeared' or were expelled from a country their labour had done much to build — all but 33,000 of the 400,000 Palestinians are now outside the country.

In Iraq itself, there was not a great deal of scope for a deterioration in human rights. What did of course happen was that as a direct result of the

Gulf War, believing themselves to be encouraged by the West, most of the 4 million Iraqi Kurds rose against Saddam Hussein and, after the military support they had been led to believe would come failed to arrive, were rapidly pushed back. Despite the safe havens established by the United Nations, thousands of people were arrested and executed. The southern marshes were bombed and napalmed, their inhabitants murdered or turned into refugees as drainage programmes destroyed their traditional marsh homes. Of the thousands of Kuwaitis taken to Iraq during the occupation, hundreds are still missing. In 1994, the Revolutionary Command Council, Iraq's highest executive body, introduced amputation, branding and execution for dozens of new offences. International outrage, heard so strongly while Kuwait was occupied, is heard no longer. There was no human rights component to the UN-sponsored ceasefire of April 1991, and none in the subsequent Memorandum of Understanding, negotiated between the UK and the Iraqi government.

The picture is no better in other countries. In Saudi Arabia, religious intolerance grows ever more extreme, with hundreds of people arrested, tortured and flogged for any form of non-Muslim worship — and even Shia Muslim worship. Executions have never been so numerous and so public. In Bahrain, a brief period of liberalisation was soon followed by intense repression, as calls for democracy led to more and more arrests. Children as young as nine are serving 10-year prison sentences for 'incitement of hatred' towards the government. Dozens of people have died during peaceful demonstrations, shot by the security forces. Bahrain consistently refuses entry to Amnesty International, on the grounds that the time is 'inappropriate'. In Bahrain, as in Syria and Tunisia, torture has become a standard part of interrogation leading to 'confession'. In Egypt, Israel and the Occupied Territories armed opposition groups are killing dozens of civilians: to fight them, suspected Islamist opponents are being rounded up, and tortured, in their thousands. In Algeria, a cycle of violence, between government forces and armed groups, has taken some 50,000 lives. There are fears now that, in the name of fighting fundamentalism, human rights are becoming the first casualty as Arab governments seize the pretext to curb all their dissidents, whatever

> **International outrage, heard so strongly while Kuwait was occupied, is heard no longer... Against fundamentalism, it would seem, all violations are legitimate**

their political or religious bent. Against fundamentalism, it would seem, all violations are legitimate. The idea of interference, which reached its most popular moment at the end of the 1980s, is now unthinkable.

No group of people, perhaps, better symbolise the collapse of human rights in the wake of the Gulf War than the 32,000 Iraqis who fled to Saudi Arabia to escape Saddam Hussein. The Saudis welcomed them as 'guests', setting up two fine camps to 'shelter' their visitors, in keeping with the traditional bonds of 'brotherhood and neighbourliness'.

There were indeed two camps, called Artawiyya and Rafha. They were put up in the northern Saudi Arabian desert, where temperatures reach 50 degrees centigrade in summer, and drop to below freezing in winter. Here the refugees were herded into makeshift tents, guarded by rotating army battalions, who patrolled with guns. From a distance, the orderly lines of double fencing and barbed wire looked a little like giant cages. In the military barracks at Artawiyya an 'emergency unit' was set up, with a tent where troublesome refugees, those fretting for a better existence, could be interrogated and sometimes tortured. There were reports of rape. *Sharia* judges ordered people found with alcohol to be flogged. Hundreds, perhaps thousands, of these refugees are thought to have been forcibly repatriated to Iraq — to probable death.

Things are said to be better now. The numbers have dropped to 15,000, Artawiyya is closed and there are regular contacts with the outside world, by post and even telephone. What hasn't changed, however, is the future: for these remaining Iraqis, doctors, lawyers, university teachers and their families, unable to go home for fear of being killed, and unwanted anywhere else, there is, at present, no future. Five years after the fighting ended, they have been forgotten.

It has now become possible to look back almost with nostalgia on the days before the Gulf War, when human rights were about violations of international treaties, when dissidents were political opponents and not terrorists, when countries acting brutally towards their citizens were called to account and where some measure of human rights was important for securing international aid and approval. In 1991 the Allies went to war for oil — but they did at least pretend it was all for human rights. Even that pretence would be inconceivable today. ❏

Caroline Moorehead is a writer and broadcaster specialising in human rights. She is currently writing a history of the International Committee of the Red Cross

LETTER FROM ACCRA

ADEWALE MAJA-PEARCE

Liberia 1996: life among the ruins of downtown Monrovia

Oscar's story

WATER was the recurring motif in Oscar's story, beginning with the leaky vessel that almost drowned him and his 3,000 compatriots. They were fleeing the latest round of savagery in Liberia's ongoing civil war, now in its sixth year, following yet another squabble between the competing 'warlords', who were busy proving themselves once again incapable of sticking to the terms of their own peace accords. At any rate, when somebody's ragtag army of boys not much older than Oscar (and some even younger) occupied their street and threatened to kill everybody in it, Oscar's parents finally agreed that their son was better entrusted to the kindness of strangers. So they scraped together the US$50 for his passage on board the Nigerian-registered ship moored off the coast of Monrovia, the capital, and bound for all ports along the West African coast; and then it transpired, soon after they put to sea, that the captain hadn't actually made arrangements to dock anywhere, and that nobody was particularly interested in giving shelter to yet more refugees. They sailed around aimlessly for 10 days until the Ghanaian authorities were finally prevailed upon by the international community to do the decent thing. Oscar said that for the last three days of his journey he was forced to drink the salt water that almost sunk them all because he could no longer afford to buy drinking water at a dollar a litre.

I met Oscar a month later. He was living in the makeshift camp in the grounds of a school and still paying for water because the camp didn't have its own supply. The local villagers charged the local refugees 30 cedis a bucket. This was cheap enough if you had the money but Oscar didn't have the money, which meant that he was forced to sell the few clothes he had come with save for the ones he now stood up in, a pair of jeans and a faded red T-shirt. Unfortunately, he had to sleep on the bare ground because he didn't have a mattress, and when it rained, which was most days at this time of year, the mud seeped under his white UNHCR tent and made him filthier. So he needed more water... As to why he didn't have a mattress, Oscar claimed that it was because the authorities in the camp had stolen all the mattresses paid for by the international community. He said that a lorry carrying brand-new mattresses had actually turned up a few days after their arrival but had left the next day without being unloaded. But that wasn't the half of it. Oscar also claimed that the authorities regularly pilfered their rations, which was why they only managed half a cup of rice a day with a little fish. He said that he tried complaining once, early on, but the soldiers beat him.

'The soldiers are always beating us,' he said, 'sometimes for no reason at all.' He said that they even beat a blind man the other day. I had seen the blind man in the camp. He was tall and thin and he was being led along the uneven path by a boy of about 10. Anyway, it was for all these reasons, Oscar said, that up to a third of the original refugees had elected to return home by road, a risky and expensive undertaking if you didn't have the proper papers. He himself was ready to leave except that he didn't have the money. Anything was better than this, he said, even the uncertainties of life in war-torn Monrovia. Here was nothing but bush and corrupt, callous officials.

These were serious allegations, of course, but how to verify them? My request to interview the refugees (and never mind the officials themselves) was turned down flat by the three policemen and the soldier I initially approached for permission when I arrived. They said that I was bound to write something which would get them all into trouble, but they wouldn't elaborate, which in itself suggested that they had something to hide. This is apart from the usual paranoia of minor officialdom in Africa, which in any case is discouraged from taking the initiative, especially when confronted by journalists. All they could suggest was that I go and see the big man in the nearby fishing town of Sekondi, but this wasn't meant to be taken seriously. In fact I should never have said anything about being a journalist except that it would have been difficult using a tape recorder without attracting attention. In the end it was easier to walk down to the main road, which marked the boundary of the camp, and simply talk to some of the refugees gathered there in small groups. That was how I met Oscar. And Oscar couldn't talk quickly enough, despite the proximity of the officials, or some of the other refugees, who could easily curry favour — a whole cup of rice, say — by reporting him. This also happened, Oscar said, but he was obviously beyond it, which made me believe him all the more. He had been waiting to tell somebody all this time because the Ghanaian media had ignored them. He said that some Ghanaian journalists had turned up on the day they docked at Takoradi but not one had bothered to come back since. So much, alas, for the kindness of strangers, to say nothing of Oscar's parents' hard-earned or begged or borrowed US$50. ❑

'Thank you very much for making it possible for our association's members to read your precious magazine...we find it interesting on many levels... "Index Index" is valuable!'
(President of the Human Rights Bureau, Morocco)

'I use *Index on Censorship* during my lessons and in general discussions with my pupils in the hope of inculcating into them the importance of freedom of expression and democratic principles.'
(Teacher, Zimbabwe)

Sponsored freedom

One of the truly innovative projects at *INDEX* is the Sponsored Subscriptions Programme, which supplies the magazine free of charge to human rights workers and organisations who can make good use of it but who are unable to subscribe themselves for financial, political or practical reasons. Recipients include lawyers, journalists and human rights workers throughout the New Independent States, Eastern Europe and the developing world. *INDEX* has proven to be a vital source material for all kinds of endeavours — for research on human rights, for teaching the importance of freedom of speech, and for reporting on issues that have not been covered in local publications around the world.

If you know of organisations in the New Independent States, Eastern Europe or the developing world which can make good use of a free subscription, please ask them to contact:

Sponsored Subscriptions Programme

Index on Censorship
Lancaster House
33 Islington High Street   Fax: 44 171 278 1878
London N1 9LH   e-mail: indexoncenso@gn.apc.org
UK   http://www.oneworld.org/index_oc/